MATT AND TOM OLDFIELD

ULTIMATE
FOOTBALL HEROES

SALAH

FROM THE PLAYGROUND
TO THE PITCH

DINO

Published by Dino Books,
an imprint of Bonnier Books UK
The Plaza,
535 Kings Road,
London, SW10 0SZ

twitter.com/dinobooks ▶
twitter.com/footieheroesbks ▶
www.heroesfootball.com

This edition published in 2018

ISBN: 978 1 78946 006 3

British Library Cataloguing-in-Publication Data:

A catalogue record for this book is available from the British Library.

Design by www.envydesign.co.uk

Printed and bound in Great Britain by Clays Ltd, Elcograf S.p.A.

7 9 10 8 6

Dino Books is an imprint of Bonnier Books UK
www.bonnierbooks.co.uk

For all readers, young and old(er)

Matt Oldfield is an accomplished writer and the editor-in-chief of football review site *Of Pitch & Page*. Tom Oldfield is a freelance sports writer and the author of biographies on Cristiano Ronaldo, Arsène Wenger and Rafael Nadal.

Cover illustration by Dan Leydon.
To learn more about Dan visit danleydon.com
To purchase his artwork visit etsy.com/shop/footynews
Or just follow him on Twitter @danleydon

TABLE OF CONTENTS

CHAPTER 1 – **EUROPEAN SUPERSTAR** 7

CHAPTER 2 – **NAGRIG** 14

CHAPTER 3 – **HEROES AND DREAMS** 19

CHAPTER 4 – **SCOUTING FOR SHERIF** 25

CHAPTER 5 – **TIRING TRAVEL** 30

CHAPTER 6 – **FIRING FOR THE FIRST TEAM** 36

CHAPTER 7 – **STAR QUALITY** 42

CHAPTER 8 – **EGYPT'S NEXT BIG THING – PART I** 48

CHAPTER 9 – **EGYPT'S NEXT BIG THING – PART II** 54

CHAPTER 10 – **GOING FOR GOLD** 61

CHAPTER 11 – **EUROPE CALLING** 66

CHAPTER 12 – **SWISS CHAMPION** 72

CHAPTER 13 – **EUROPEAN STAR** 78

CHAPTER 14 – **LONDON CALLING** 86

CHAPTER 15 – **WORLD CUP DREAM – PART I** 93

CHAPTER 16 – **CHANCES AT CHELSEA** 98

CHAPTER 17 – **FIRING AGAIN AT FIORENTINA** 104

CHAPTER 18 – **ROARING AT ROMA** 111

CHAPTER 19 – **AFRICAN CUP OF NATIONS** 118

CHAPTER 20 – **MOHAMED AND EDIN** 126

CHAPTER 21 – **WORLD CUP DREAM – PART II** 131

CHAPTER 22 – **LIVERPOOL** 140

CHAPTER 23 – **PREMIER LEAGUE PLAYER OF THE YEAR** . . 149

CHAPTER 1

EUROPEAN SUPERSTAR

Anfield, 24 April 2018

The atmosphere at Anfield was always amazing but on big European nights, it was extra special. The chorus of the Kop started hours before kick-off and, if Liverpool were to beat Roma, it would go on for days afterwards. The fans sang the old favourites like 'You'll Never Walk Alone', and they sang the new favourites too:

Mo Salah, Mo Salah
Running down the wing,
Salah la la la la la la
Egyptian King!

The eyes of the world were on Liverpool's

'Egyptian King'. Mohamed was in the best form of his life, with forty goals and counting. He had already scored thirty-one in the Premier League and nine in the Champions League. Could he keep shooting his team all the way to the final?

For Mohamed, it was going to be an emotional night, no matter what. First of all, he was playing in his first-ever Champions League semi-final, a moment that he had dreamed about ever since he was an eight-year-old boy. He was following in the footsteps of his heroes like Zinedine Zidane and Francesco Totti.

Mohamed was also playing against his old club. When his big move to Chelsea hadn't worked out, it was Italian football that saved him. At Fiorentina, and then Roma, he had rediscovered his passion, his confidence, and the path to superstardom. He would always be grateful for that.

Mohamed's old manager, Luciano Spalletti, had moved on, but lots of his old teammates were still there – Radja Nainggolan, Stephan El Shaarawy, and his old strike partner, Edin Džeko. In the tunnel,

Mohamed hugged each and every one of them.

'Good luck,' he said with a smile, 'may the best team win!'

Liverpool were far from a one-man team. Mohamed was one part of 'The Big Three', the hottest strikeforce in the world. With Sadio Mané on the left, Roberto Firmino in the middle, and Mohamed on the right, the Reds looked unstoppable. Even Philippe Coutinho's move to Barcelona hadn't slowed them down. They had scored five against Porto in the Round of 16 and then five against Manchester City in the quarter-finals too. If the Roma defenders weren't careful, 'The Big Three' would run riot again.

'Come on lads, let's win this!' the Liverpool captain Jordan Henderson shouted as the players took up their positions for kick-off.

Even during his days at Roma, Mohamed had been more of a winger than a striker. With his amazing sprint speed, he would race past defenders and set up chances for Edin. At Liverpool, however, manager Jürgen Klopp had helped turn Mohamed into a proper forward and a goalscoring machine. He still worked hard for his team but he did it higher up the pitch. That way, if a defender made a mistake, he was always ready to pounce.

Liverpool created their first good opening after twenty-seven minutes. One clever flick from Roberto was all it took to set speedy Sadio away. He had Mohamed to his right but Sadio wanted the glory for himself. In the penalty area, he pulled back his left foot and… blazed it over the crossbar!

The Liverpool fans buried their heads in their hands – what a missed opportunity! Two minutes later, another one arrived. Mohamed played a great pass to Roberto, who squared it to Sadio. He hit it first time… high and wide!

Groans rang out around Anfield. They couldn't keep wasting these opportunities! Liverpool needed more composure in front of goal. What they needed was a cool head…

Sadio passed to Roberto, who passed to Mohamed on the right side of the box. With a quick tap of the boot, he shifted the ball onto his lethal left foot. Time to shoot? No, not quite yet. Mohamed took one more touch to get a better angle, and then curled a fierce strike into the top corner. The technique was astonishing and he made it look so easy.

Gooooooooooooooooooooaaaaaaaaaaaaaaaallllllllllll llllllllllllllll!!!!!!!!!!!!!!!!!!

Mohamed put his arms up straight away – he wasn't going to celebrate a goal against his old team. That didn't stop the Liverpool fans, though, or his new teammates.

'Get in!' Jordan screamed, punching the air.

In the last minute of the first half, Mohamed passed to Roberto near the halfway line and sprinted forward for the one-two. The Roma defenders had no chance of catching him. Instead, their goalkeeper rushed out to the edge of his area to block the shot but Mohamed lifted the ball delicately over him. So calm and so classy! As it rolled into the back of the net, he lifted his arms up again.

Gooooooooooooooooooooaaaaaaaaaaaaaaaallllllllllll llllllllllllllll!!!!!!!!!!!!!!!!!!

There was just no stopping Mohamed. In the

second half, he beat Roma's offside trap again and crossed to Sadio for a simple tap-in. *3–0!*

They pointed over at Roberto. 'Bobby, it's your turn to score now!'

Mohamed picked the ball up on the right wing and attacked the poor Roma left-back, who backed away in fear. Hadn't Mohamed done enough damage for one day? No! He danced his way through and crossed to Roberto at the back post. *4–0!*

Liverpool's 'Big Three' were all on the scoresheet yet again. It was party time at Anfield:

We've got Salah, do do do do do do!

Mané Mané, do do do do do,

And Bobby Firmino,

And we sold Coutinho!

After seventy-five brilliant minutes, Klopp gave his superstar a well-deserved rest. As Mohamed left the pitch, both sets of fans stood up to clap his world-class performance, and the humble hero clapped right back.

At Basel, Mohamed had become a European star; at Liverpool, he had become a European *super*star.

With two great goals and two amazing assists, Mohamed had led Liverpool towards the Champions League final, just as he had led his country, Egypt, to the 2018 World Cup.

'So, just how good *is* Mohamed Salah?' the TV presenter asked.

Liverpool legend Steven Gerrard smiled and replied: 'He's the best player on the planet right now!'

That had always been Mohamed's dream, ever since he first kicked a football on his local pitch in Nagrig.

CHAPTER 2

NAGRIG

'Come on!' Mohamed Salah called out impatiently to his brother. 'The others will be waiting!'

'Coming!' Nasr replied, his voice echoing down the corridor. He quickly pushed his feet into his shoes and slammed the front door behind him.

The Salah brothers didn't have far to go. Nagrig was a small farming village in Egypt, with only one main dusty street cutting through wide fields of green and yellow. Around that one main dusty street, however, was everything that they needed – their home, their school, the shop, the post office, the café, the community centre and the mosque.

Most importantly of all, tucked in between the

crumbling blocks of flats and the community centre, was their football pitch. It was the same football pitch that their dad and uncles had played on when they were young boys. The surface was bone dry and bobbly but there was a rusty set of goalposts and plenty of space to play.

'Hey, wait for me!' Nasr shouted as he chased after his older brother.

With a loud sigh, Mohamed slowed down to let him catch up. That was their parents' one condition; the two boys could go out and play as much football as they liked, just as long as Mohamed looked after Nasr.

When they arrived at the pitch, they found a group of boys sitting sadly in the goalmouth. They had no football, so what were they supposed to do?

Fortunately, Mohamed and Nasr had brought one.

'Finally!' the other boys called out, jumping up and dusting down their shorts. 'Yeah, pass it over here!'

Mohamed kicked the ball to them and they took it in turns to shoot. The goal didn't have a net, but the ball bounced back off the low wall around the pitch. The boys knew to keep everything under head height. They had learnt this lesson the hard way.

'Hey! What do you think you're doing?'

High shots had a horrible habit of landing in the surrounding flats. Sometimes they just got a telling-off; sometimes, they didn't get the ball back. It all depended on the damage done and the mood of the neighbour. So, it was best to aim low and hard instead.

'Right, let's pick teams!' Mohamed declared. After a few kicks, he was warmed up and ready to go. What were they waiting for?

'You can have Nasr, Abu and Khalid, okay?' decided Mahmoud, the eldest boy.

Mohamed nodded and tried to look happy. He would need to be at his very best because this was the worst team possible! His brother was the youngest and the smallest, while Ahmed and Khalid weren't exactly natural footballers.

'You can have kick-off!' Mahmoud offered.

'Wow, how kind of you!' Mohamed muttered to himself.

It was a good thing that he was feeling determined. When Ahmed passed the ball back to him, Mohamed came alive. He dribbled forward at full speed, keeping the ball glued to his left foot. Three opponents eventually stopped him, but they still couldn't get it off him. With all attention focused on him, Mohamed slipped a pass through to Nasr. 1–0!

'Come on, guys!' Mahmoud moaned, throwing his arms up in the air.

Mohamed, on the other hand, didn't say a word. He just high-fived his brother and got ready to defend. They had a battle on their hands.

Mahmoud's team scored lots of goals, but they just couldn't cope with Mohamed's trickery. Every time he got the ball, he found a new way to get his team a goal. Sometimes it was a turn and shot; sometimes it was a stepover and a burst of speed; and sometimes it was a clever pass or cross.

'Right, half-time!' Mahmoud panted, sitting down in the shade.

But Mohamed didn't want the fun to stop.

While the others rested, he carried on practising his skills. When he played football, everything else disappeared, especially the poverty and decay around him. He allowed himself to dream of a better life as a superstar footballer. He loved Nagrig, but how cool would it be to travel the world and become an international hero?

'You're going to be a big player one day,' his friends were always telling him.

But as soon as he stopped kicking a ball, that dream seemed silly. How was he ever going to become a superstar footballer when even Cairo, Egypt's capital city, felt like a million miles away?

CHAPTER 3

HEROES AND DREAMS

At the café in Nagrig, Mohamed found his first gateway to the stars – a TV screen that showed foreign football matches. As long as the boys bought a drink or two to share, they were allowed to stay and watch until their parents called them home.

'Please Mum, there's only about ten minutes to go!' they often lied.

Mohamed stared up at that magical TV screen for hours and hours. He watched great games from the Spanish, Italian and English leagues but his favourite was the Champions League, Europe's top club competition.

He was always looking for new tricks to learn and

new players to copy. Mohamed loved entertaining attackers who liked to show off their silky skills. His top heroes were Ryan Giggs at Manchester United, Zinedine Zidane at Real Madrid, and Francesco Totti at Roma.

'Whoa, did you see that?' Mohamed would call out excitedly, his eyes wide with awe.

The next day, he would become his Champions League heroes out on the football pitch. Mohamed's plan was to practise and practise until he could dribble like Giggs, pass like Zidane and shoot like Totti. He was only nine years old, so there was still plenty of time.

'Just you wait!' Mohamed told his friends, and no-one argued with his ambition.

Egypt didn't play at the 2002 World Cup in Japan and South Korea, but the African continent was otherwise well-represented: Egypt's neighbours Tunisia had qualified for the tournament, and so had Nigeria, Cameroon and Senegal. Senegal faced Zidane's France in the tournament's very first match. Everyone expected them to lose but after thirty minutes, Papa Bouba Diop scrambled the ball into the net to stun the World Champions. 1–0 to Senegal!

It was a footballing moment that Mohamed would never forget. An African nation had beaten France! It felt like a whole world of opportunities had opened up. If Senegal could do it, why not Egypt? Mohamed dared to dream. If he kept getting better and better, perhaps one day he could lead his country to glory.

'One day,' he promised himself. World Cup fever had well and truly arrived in Nagrig.

The 2002 tournament also gave Mohamed three new idols – Brazil's '3Rs', Ronaldo, Rivaldo and Ronaldinho. Together, the trio had it all: pace, power, skills, *and* goals. Not only were they fun to watch, but they also went on to win the World Cup trophy, beating Germany in the final.

'Today, I'm going to be Ronaldo!' Mohamed declared as he walked out on to the local football pitch.

Mohamed was totally hooked on football. It was all he thought about and all he talked about too.

What would he need to do in order to follow in the footsteps of his heroes? That was his dream and he was determined to achieve it, no matter what.

Ghamry Abdel Hamid El Saadany, the local youth club coach, did his best to develop Mohamed's skills but there was only so much help he could offer. By the age of twelve, Mohamed was already in a league of his own. No-one in Nagrig had ever seen such footballing talent.

'He's got fire in his eyes, and fire in his boots too!' the spectators noted.

'That kid's going to Egypt's next superstar!' they predicted.

It was clear that the local league was far too easy for Mohamed. As he glided across the pitch, the defenders just backed away in fear, surrendering without a fight. He scored goal after goal after goal.

'Your talent is wasted here,' Mohamed's dad eventually told him after yet another match-winning performance. 'We need to find you a new challenge!'

Salah Ghaly decided to take his son for a trial at Ittihad Basyoun, a bigger and better club, based half an hour away. For the first time ever, Mohamed would have to play with new teammates, boys that he hadn't even met before, let alone known all his life.

'I can do this!' he told himself, shaking away his nerves and shyness.

This was only the first step in Mohamed's football journey. If he couldn't pass this test, how was he going to go on and play in the Champions League and the World Cup?

'Good luck!' his dad called out to him, but his head was already in the game.

During the warm-up, Mohamed kicked a ball around on his own, listening to the others laughing together. As the new kid in town, he was going to have to prove himself before he could join their gang.

'I can do this!' he repeated to himself under his breath.

In the skills drills, Mohamed was solid but not spectacular. He was saving his explosive burst for the match at the end. Dribbling through cones wasn't the same as dribbling through defenders. It didn't give him the same incredible buzz. Nothing else did.

Mohamed took up a position on the left wing and waited for the ball. He was like a sportscar, coasting in third gear but ready to speed off at the slightest touch of the accelerator.

Zoom! When the pass finally arrived, Mohamed was off, weaving his way towards goal with his lethal left foot. Nobody in Nagrig could stop him, and neither could the boys of Ittihad Basyoun. As he slid the ball past the goalkeeper, his opponents just stood there in shock. It was their first experience of Mohamed's trickery, but it certainly wouldn't be their last.

'Wow, great goal!' his new teammates said, giving him high-fives. Now that they had seen him in action, they all wanted to be his friend.

That one training session was enough to convince the Ittihad Basyoun coach.

'Welcome to the team!' he said, shaking Mohamed's hand.

CHAPTER 4

SCOUTING FOR SHERIF

Being a football scout in Egypt wasn't easy. Reda El-Mallah spent long hours on the road, driving to tiny sports centres in faraway villages aiming to discover the 'next big thing'. For every success story, there were hundreds of disappointed hopefuls.

Many of Egypt's top clubs were based around the capital city, Cairo, but there was footballing talent to be found all over the country, often in the most unlikely places. You just had to know where to look for it, and El-Mallah was a man in the know. Youth coaches were always calling him, telling him to come and check out their latest prospect.

'Okay, when's your next game?' he would reply. He

loved the excitement of it all, the thrill of the chase.

On this particular day, El-Mallah was on his way to Nagrig to check out a young player called Sherif. He didn't know much about him, but that didn't matter. The scout knew what to look for, the signs of a superstar.

When he arrived in the village, the local coach met him and pointed out Sherif in a crowd of boys. He looked tall, strong and athletic, but then so did lots of youngsters. Was he actually any good at football? That was the key question and there was only one way to find out.

'Right, I'm going to need to see him in action,' El-Mallah said, standing on the sidelines.

The coach quickly organised the boys into two teams and told them to get started. The game was supposed to showcase Sherif's talent, but it was another player who stole the limelight.

Mohamed had just come down to his local pitch for a casual kickabout as usual. Although he was happy playing for his new club Ittihad Basyoun, he was always aiming higher. When he heard that a top scout had come to watch, he dared to dream. This could be his ticket to the top.

'Apparently, he works for El Mokawloon!' the rumour spread around the group in excited whispers.

El Mokawloon was a club in Cairo, playing in the Egyptian Premier League. What an opportunity! On the outside, Mohamed looked as calm as ever but, on the inside, his heart was racing. This was the big moment that he'd been waiting for. He was determined to make the most of it.

As soon as the game kicked off, Mohamed was on the ball and looking for ways to impress. Yes, he could do lots of tricks and flicks, but he didn't want to look like a show-off in front of the scout. He was a team player, and so after dribbling like Giggs, he passed like Zidane, and then moved into space to get it back. Only once he was within scoring distance did Mohamed shoot like Totti. *Bang!* He unleashed his lethal left foot and the ball flew past the goalkeeper.

Goooooooooooooooooooaaaaaaaaaaaaaaaalllllllllll llllllllllllll!!!!!!!!!!!!!!!!!

At first, El-Mallah stuck to his task of watching

Sherif. The problem was, however, that he was hardly touching the ball. It was another, smaller boy who was running the show. Every time this kid got the ball, the game came to life. He played with such energy and excitement that El-Mallah couldn't help watching him instead.

'What a finish!' he muttered to himself when Mohamed scored his first goal.

El-Mallah was impressed by Mohamed's attitude too. He didn't celebrate like a superstar, or shout or sulk. He was quiet, hard-working and modest. The other players weren't working *for* him; they were working *with* him, together as a team.

By the time Mohamed completed his hat-trick, El-Mallah had forgotten all about Sherif.

'Look at that speed!' he marvelled.

'Look at that touch!'

'Look at that skill!'

Mohamed was enjoying himself so much that he forgot all about the scout. He was doing what he loved – playing football for fun. It just so happened that he was very, very good at it.

After blowing the final whistle, the coach went over to speak to El-Mallah. 'So, what did you think of Sherif?'

'Sherif?' the scout replied. For a moment, he looked confused until he remembered the name. 'Oh yes, Sherif! No, I'm afraid that he's not the one I'm interested in.'

'What's *his* name?' El-Mallah asked, pointing straight at Mohamed. 'He's the real deal!'

Within weeks, Mohamed signed for a youth team in Tanta, a city located ninety minutes away from Nagrig. They were a bigger club who played at a higher level, but that didn't faze Mohamed one bit. He took everything in his stride and, following a string of excellent performances there, he next signed for El Mokawloon.

'No way, I can't believe this is really happening!' Mohamed screamed with joy.

El-Mallah had come to Nagrig, scouting for Sherif. Instead, he had found Mohamed and the fourteen-year-old boy's impossible dream was now about to come true.

CHAPTER 5

TIRING TRAVEL

For Mohamed, there was only really one downside to playing for El Mokawloon, and that was the journey to and from the club. It was based in Cairo, a massive four-and-a-half-hour journey from Nagrig. The Salah family couldn't just drop everything and move to the capital city for the sake of their son's football career. So, how was Mohamed going to get there?

The El Mokawloon youth team didn't just train once a week; they trained FIVE times a week! His dad drove him to his first few sessions, but after that, Mohamed had to make his own way there and back. He had always known that becoming a professional footballer was going to be tough, but he hadn't expected the bus rides to be the biggest challenge.

'This is ridiculous!' he complained at first, but he soon got used to the tiring travel.

Mohamed's normal school day started at seven in the morning and was over by nine.

His friends were so jealous of the special permission slip that El Mokawloon had given him. 'You only have to do two hours of class per day?' they would say. 'That's not fair – I wish I was a football superstar!'

It wasn't all fun and games, though. The journey to Cairo could be lonely and difficult, especially for a fourteen-year-old who was used to small-village life. To get there, Mohamed had to switch buses three times, maybe more if there were any problems. Sometimes they were so crowded that he had to climb in through the windows. Mohamed would do anything to make it to football. If he missed any of his connections or the buses were running late, it was a total disaster.

By the time he arrived for the afternoon training session, Mohamed was usually stressed and tired,

and yet his football day was only just beginning.
After changing into his kit, he had a few minutes to
calm himself down and get his head into the game.
He wasn't playing local league football anymore; this
was serious stuff at Egypt's highest level. If Mohamed
wasn't 110 per cent focused, he could forget about a
professional contract.

'Faster!' the coaches called out, pushing him to his
limits. 'Stronger!'

Four fun but gruelling hours later, Mohamed
was back on the bus to Nagrig. He was exhausted,
hungry, and he still had homework to do. When he
finally got home, he wolfed down a quick dinner and
then went straight to bed. On really bad days, that
could be as late as 1a.m. When he woke up, it was
time to do it all over again.

'What's it like at El Mokawloon?' Nasr sometimes
tried to ask his sleepy brother over breakfast, but he
never got much of an answer.

'Okay, maybe I don't wish I was a football
superstar!' his friends admitted when Mohamed
explained his daily routine.

It would all be worth it in the end, however, as long as he kept on progressing. When El Mokawloon called him up to their senior squad, Mohamed would get his own room to stay in, right next to the Osman Ahmed Osman Stadium. Then, all that tiring travel would stop.

Mohamed was learning fast and doing everything that the coaches asked of him. When he had first arrived at El Mokawloon, they had given him the Number 3 shirt and asked him to play at left-back.

'You've made a mistake – I'm not a defender!' Mohamed thought to himself, but he didn't argue out loud. There was a lot of competition for the team's attacking roles and he would have to prove himself first, just as he had done in Basyoun and Tanta. Until then, he would just have to do his best for his new team, while trying to get forward as much as possible.

Thankfully, Hamdi Nooh, the youth coach, soon realised that Mohamed was playing out of position. After an important 4–0 victory, he found the youngster in tears in the dressing room.

'What's wrong, kid?' Nooh asked. 'You just thrashed those guys!'

Mohamed sniffed and wiped his eyes with his shirt. 'It's nothing, I just really wanted to score today, and I didn't.'

'But you're a defender, aren't you?'

Mohamed shook his head. 'I was a winger until I came here. I'm trying to attack like I used to, but it's hard when I have to keep tracking back.'

Nooh listened carefully and then paused for thought. Finally he said: 'Thanks for being so honest with me, Mo. I had no idea that you cared so much about goals! Here's what we're going to do – next week, you're going to play in attack and we'll see how you get on.'

That moment was the making of Mohamed. As soon as he was back where he belonged, he scored goal after goal and El Mokawloon won game after game.

'Not bad for a left-back!' Nooh liked to joke with him.

In order to defeat the best defenders, Mohamed

added extra strength to go with his speed and skill. It was now even harder to get the ball off him, as he dribbled towards goal. Mohamed could feel his first-team target getting closer and closer with every passing day. The thought kept him going during those boring bus rides.

'I can do this!' he told himself.

Mohamed was determined to be something special, no matter what. Football was his chosen talent, his gateway to the stars.

CHAPTER 6

FIRING FOR THE FIRST TEAM

'RIGHT FOOT!' Nooh bellowed out across the
El Mokawloon training pitch. All the youth players
stopped, hoping that their coach was shouting at
someone else. 'You've got one, haven't you? Well,
use it then!'

His anger was aimed at Mohamed, who had just
dribbled the ball straight off the pitch with his left
foot, instead of cutting inside onto his weaker right.
El Mokawloon's young star stared down at the grass
for a second and then chased back to make up for
his mistake.

Nooh refused to go easy on Mohamed, even
when he scored thirty-five goals in one season for

the Under-16s and Under-17s. He wasn't there just to praise his players; he was there to help the best become even better.

'Superstars never stop improving,' the academy coach explained after the session. 'You're lightning-quick and your left foot is lethal but what's your Plan B? What's your Plan C? As an attacker, you need to have lots of different options to choose from. That way, you keep the defender guessing!'

Mohamed nodded enthusiastically. 'Thanks Coach, I'll work hard on my right foot.'

'I know you will!' Nooh replied with a smile.

Mohamed was the ideal student, eager to learn and determined to succeed. A week later, he found himself in a very similar position again. As he raced down the left wing, the defender blocked his path, trying to push him inside onto his weaker side.

'I can do this!' Mohamed told himself. Since his chat with Nooh, he had spent every spare moment practising. It was time to put his training to the test.

With a drop of the left shoulder, Mohamed tapped the ball across to the right. He had fooled the defender and created space for a shot… with his rubbish right foot. Did he have time to switch it back to his lethal left? No, his right foot wasn't rubbish anymore! He had to believe in himself. Besides, if he got it wrong in a practice match, so what? *Bang!*

Goooooooooooooooooooaaaaaaaaaaaaaaaalllllllllll llllllllllllll!!!!!!!!!!!!!!!!!!!

'EXCELLENT, much better!' Nooh clapped and cheered.

This time, his player deserved the praise. Mohamed had the attitude of a professional footballer and he had the talent to match it.

'How is my son doing?' Salah Ghaly called up to ask one day.

'Very well,' Nooh was pleased to report. 'Mohamed is going to be a great player one day and play at the highest level.'

It was now a question of 'when', rather than 'if'. As the 2009–10 Egyptian Premier League season drew to a close, El Mokawloon were down in the bottom half of the table, a massive thirty points behind the leaders, Al Ahly. That was a familiar position for 'The Mountain Wolves'. They had only ever won the league once, way back in 1983.

No, El Mokawloon weren't chasing titles but they did have a proud record of giving their young players the chance to shine. That's why Mohamed stayed at the club and that's why another Mohamed – Mohamed Elneny – decided to join from Al Ahly. The Two Mohameds quickly became best friends. They shared the same big dream:

'We're going to break into the first team together and become international superstars!'

Mohamed Salah was one step closer to achieving that ambition. He was already training with El Mokawloon's senior squad, where he had impressed the assistant coach, Mohamed 'Zizo' Abdelaziz.

'Let's give him a go,' he argued with the manager. 'The kid is still raw but he's really exciting! What have we got to lose?'

With three games to go, Mohamed was named as a substitute for El Mokawloon's trip to El-Mansoura. When he heard the news, it was the proudest moment of his young life. He wanted to jump into Zizo's arms.

'Thank you, thank you!' Mohamed cried out joyfully. 'You won't regret this, I promise!'

The assistant coach tried to keep him calm. 'Don't get your hopes up just yet, okay? You might not even come on.'

But with fifteen minutes to go at the El-Mansoura Stadium, the score was still 1–1. The game needed a spark of life, a super sub.

'Salah!' Zizo called out to the bench behind him. 'Go get warmed up.'

Mohamed jumped to his feet and jogged along the touchline. He tried to slow his heartbeat down a little with some long, deep breaths, but one look up at the crowd and it was racing again. What an atmosphere!

This was it, the moment that he had longed for ever since his first footballing days in Nagrig. He was about to make his debut in the Egyptian Premier League at the age of sixteen! With hard work and dedication, that impossible dream had become possible.

Wearing the Number 31 shirt, Mohamed chased after every goalscoring chance. In a race against

El-Mansouras' tired defenders, there was only
ever going to be one winner. The El Mokawloon
fans loved his energy and encouraged him to keep
dribbling with the ball.

Take him on! Use your skills!

Mohamed didn't score but he showed enough
potential to keep his place on the bench for the
last two games of the season. He played another
ten minutes against ENPPI and then a whole thirty
minutes against PetroJet.

'So, how does it feel?' his friend Elneny asked. He
wanted to know every detail about the experience.

'Mate, it feels incredible, like you could just keep
running for days!'

Mohamed's tiring travel times were over. Now
that he was a first-team player, he finally had his
own room right next to the Osman Ahmed Osman
Stadium. From there, he could plan the next step on
his journey to the top.

'You and I are going to take the league by storm!'
he told Elneny.

CHAPTER 7

STAR QUALITY

Mohamed prepared for his first full season at El
Mokawloon in the same way that he prepared
for everything – with practice, practice and more
practice.

He worked on his right foot,

He worked on his left foot,

He worked on his strength,

He worked on his shooting,

He even worked on his speed!

'We need to make the most of that amazing sprint
of yours,' Zizo told him at the start of the summer.

Zizo's new protégé displayed a kind of exciting
combination of talent, drive and discipline that he

had never encountered before. Mohamed was a rare jewel who just needed a bit of care and polish.

'Mark my words – that kid has real star quality!' the coach told everyone, including the player himself. He knew that Mohamed was too humble to let the praise go to his head.

Together, they came up with a brand new plan of attack – run more, dribble less.

'At the moment, you're holding onto the ball for too long,' Zizo explained. 'It's fun to watch but it invites defenders to tackle – or foul – you. If you released it earlier, though, you could then use your speed to burst behind the defence for the one-two. Think how many goals you could score that way!'

Mohamed listened carefully and eagerly to his coach. Any plan involving more goals sounded good to him. 'Let's do it!' he agreed.

Nooh's message – 'Superstars never stop improving' – was still there at the front of Mohamed's mind. He wasn't too old to have heroes to look up to. That summer he watched Ronaldo, Messi and Andrés Iniesta at the 2010 World Cup.

'That's going to be me one day!' Mohamed promised to himself.

An African nation had made it to the World Cup quarter-finals again, this time Michael Essien's Ghana. Soon, it would be Egypt's turn.

Before all that, however, the Two Mohameds needed to take the national league by storm. By December 2010, they were both first-team regulars, Elneny in midfield and Salah in attack. The only problem was that El Mokawloon were losing almost every match. It was going to take a miracle to lift the club up the league table.

'Hey, come on, we can do this!' they tried to tell their teammates.

Mohamed Salah was feeling particularly confident. He had finally scored his first goal in the Egyptian Cup against Suez, and now it was time to score in the Egyptian Premier League too. On Christmas Day, El Mokawloon took on the champions, Al Ahly, at the International Stadium.

Mohamed could hear Zizo in his head, telling him to 'make the most of that amazing sprint of yours'.

That wasn't easy against such a top team, but he didn't give up. All he needed was one opportunity...

By the time his teammate played the long pass over the top, Mohamed was already on the run. The surprised Al Ahly defenders had no chance of catching up with him.

Mohamed controlled the ball on the edge of the penalty area and then steadied himself for the shot, just like Nooh and Zizo had taught him. This was that one chance he'd been waiting for; he had to make it count. Out of the corner of his eye, he could see a defender approaching but he didn't panic. Instead, Mohamed fired the ball straight past the goalkeeper.

Goooooooooooooooooooooaaaaaaaaaaaaaaaaaallllllllllll llllllllllllllll!!!!!!!!!!!!!!!!!!!

With a big smile on his face, he put a finger to his lips to cheekily shush the stunned Al Ahly supporters. They had underestimated Mohamed, something that the El Mokawloon fans had never done. Even though he was still only a raw seventeen-year-old, they always believed in him.

'That's for you!' he told them with a wave.

Then Mohamed bent down and kissed the grass below his feet. It was the best moment of his life, and he had so much to be thankful for. He was one of the lucky ones who got to live out his dreams on the football pitch.

El Mokawloon's results weren't really improving, but their two young stars certainly were. After Mohamed Elneny scored twice against Zamalek one week, Mohamed Salah scored twice against Smouha the following week.

His first goal was a powerful poke with the outside of his left boot, and his second was straight out of Zizo's training ground exercises. Mohamed got the ball in his own half and passed it quickly forward to the central striker. Then he was off, making the most of his amazing sprint speed. When the return pass arrived, he just had one last defender to beat before lifting his shot over the diving goalkeeper.

Gooooooooooooooooooooaaaaaaaaaaaaaaaallllllllllll llllllllllllll!!!!!!!!!!!!!!!!!

It wasn't just a goal; it was a wondergoal, the kind he used to score at the pitch in Nagrig. Mohamed stood in front of the fans and lifted his arms up in the air. Wow, this was what it felt like to be a hero.

'I love it!' he cheered loudly. Now, he just needed to learn to do it week in, week out.

Sadly, the Two Mohameds still couldn't rescue El Mokawloon's season. After all their hard work, it was heartbreaking to finish bottom of the league. Luckily, they weren't relegated to the Second Division.

'You're our most important players now,' Zizo told the Two Mohameds during the summer of 2011. 'I know you're still very young, but this is the time to step up and be our heroes. I know you can do it!'

CHAPTER 8

EGYPT'S NEXT BIG THING – PART I

Before the new club season, however, the Two
Mohameds were off to represent their country of
Egypt at the 2011 Under-20 World Cup in Colombia.
They couldn't wait to go on the trip of a lifetime.

'There will be scouts from all over the world
watching!' Elneny predicted.

'Yes, and we even get to play against Brazil!' Salah
added, thinking back to the 'Three Rs' at the 2002
World Cup – Ronaldo, Rivaldo and Ronaldinho.

Egypt would definitely be one of the underdogs
in South America, but they deserved their place
at the tournament. They had made it to the semi-
finals of the African Youth Championships in South

Africa, beating Mali 1–0 in the third-place playoff.

Now, it was time for Egypt's new Golden Generation to test themselves against the world's best footballing nations. Mohamed Salah was looking forward to the challenge. Although he had played well at the African Youth Championships, he had only scored one goal in five games.

'And that was just a penalty!' he reminded his teammate Ahmed Hegazi. 'I can do so much better than that.'

Mohamed wasn't the captain, but he was Egypt's 'next big thing'. He was the team's top attacking talent, their only player with real star quality. His country was counting on him, especially against Brazil, whose team was full of future superstars like Philippe Coutinho, Oscar, Casemiro and Danilo.

'We should remember these names,' Ahmed joked. 'They'll all be playing in the English Premier League soon!'

Mohamed laughed along but, in his head, he was thinking, 'Why couldn't *we* be the ones playing in the English Premier League soon?' As long as they kept believing and improving, there was nothing stopping them.

In the twelfth minute of the game, Coutinho crossed and Danilo headed in. 1–0 to Brazil! Egypt, however, came back fighting. Instead of panicking, they passed the ball around patiently. Fifteen minutes later, Omar Gaber scored the equaliser. 1–1! The whole squad celebrated together on the touchline, including the substitutes and the coaches.

'We deserved that!' Mohamed shouted to his teammates. 'We've been the better team!'

Egypt were unlucky not to win but a draw against Brazil was an excellent way to start the tournament. If they could beat Panama, they had a real chance of qualifying for the second round. For Mohamed, though, that turned out to be another frustrating game. A cross deflected off a defender but bounced back off the post. His lethal left foot fired a shot just over the crossbar.

'Nooooo!' he cried out, swiping at the warm afternoon air.

Mohamed was so desperate to score and become

the national hero, but it was Ahmed who popped up with the winning header in the second half. The Egypt players bent down and kissed the grass together.

Against Austria, Mohamed Ibrahim scored a hat-trick in a 4–0 thrashing. For Mohamed Salah, however, the goal drought continued. What was he doing wrong? Was he trying too hard?

The Egypt coach Diaa El-Sayed thought so. 'You're playing well, Mo, and we're winning games! I know you love scoring but there's a lot more to your game than that. You're our creator, our playmaker. The goals will only come when you stop thinking about them so much.'

Mohamed knew that his manager was right. He wasn't a selfish striker, so why did he care so much about goals? He just needed to focus on doing his best for the team, for Egypt.

In the Round of 16, they were up against Argentina. They didn't have anyone to rival Messi but Érik Lamela was still a very dangerous opponent.

'Stay strong and stay clever!' El-Sayed warned his players.

In the closing minutes of a tense first half, Mohamed tracked Carlos Luque back into his own box and accidentally clipped his heels. He held up his hands to show that he was innocent, but the referee still pointed to the spot. Penalty!

Mohamed couldn't believe it. He was trying to help his team but instead, he had just made things worse. He walked away in disgust, unable to watch as Lamela scored.

'Right, I need to make up for my mistake,' he told himself as the match kicked off again.

Before he could do that, however, Argentina won another penalty and Lamela scored again. 2–0! It looked like game over, but Mohamed wasn't ready to give up just yet, especially not at his first international tournament. When Egypt were awarded the third penalty of the match, he sprinted over to grab the ball.

'I've got this!' Mohamed called out confidently.

There was no way that he would let anyone else take it. He stood on the edge of the area with his hands on his hips, waiting for the referee's whistle.

He didn't let a single doubt creep into his head. This spot-kick was going in. When it blew, he stepped up and calmly sent the goalkeeper the wrong way. 2–1!

Goooooooooooooooooooaaaaaaaaaaaaaaaalllllllllll llllllllllll!!!!!!!!!!!!!!!!!!!

'Come on!' Mohamed cheered as he grabbed the ball and raced back for the restart. 'We've still got time!'

Sadly, Egypt couldn't find the second goal that they needed, and they were knocked out of the competition in that second round. As the Argentina players celebrated, Mohamed sank to the grass in a daze of disappointment.

It was one of the worst moments of Mohamed's career. He had arrived in South America with such high hopes for his team, and for himself. There had been moments of magic but overall, he felt like he had failed. He only had one goal to show for all his efforts – a penalty kick.

'Keep your head up, kid,' El-Sayed told him, patting him on the back. 'It's all about how you learn from this experience. Use that hurt to lead Egypt to the World Cup one day!'

CHAPTER 9

EGYPT'S NEXT BIG THING – PART II

Before he could even lead Egypt to a World Cup tournament, Mohamed had to break into his country's senior team. That wasn't going to be easy, though. The Egypt coach Hassan Shehata didn't like taking risks with youngsters. He preferred to pick players with plenty of experience. Essam El-Hadary had more than 100 caps and Ahmed Hassan had more than 170! Furthermore, the average age of the squad that won the 2010 African Cup of Nations was twenty-seven, and Mohamed was much much younger.

'I'm not waiting another eight years for my chance!' Mohamed declared.

Mohamed, Elneny, Ahmed, Omar – there was a

whole generation of exciting young players coming through and they couldn't be ignored forever.

In September 2011, when Mohamed was nineteen years old, they finally got their chance. New manager Hany Ramzy selected Egypt's Under-23s to play in the African Cup of Nations qualifiers against Sierra Leone and Niger. This was their huge opportunity to impress. Could they make the most of it?

'I've never felt so old in all my life,' Ahmed Hassan joked. He was the only senior player left in the side. 'Forget father figure; I'm more like a grandfather figure!'

Despite their team spirit, Egypt's new-look line-up got off to an awful start in Sierra Leone. Elneny sliced a clearance into his own net.

'Don't worry, keep going!' Mohamed Salah comforted his devastated friend. He was going to do everything possible to save the day for Egypt.

Mohamed Salah ran and ran, looking for that goalscoring chance. Just before half-time, he got the ball on the right wing and dribbled infield. The Sierra Leone defenders just stood back and watched.

What a terrible mistake! He was a long way out, but Mohamed could shoot from anywhere with his lethal left foot. *Bang!*

The ball flew towards the bottom corner and bounced up awkwardly in front of the goalkeeper. All he could do was push it away and Marwan Mohsen was there to score the rebound. 1–1!

'Great work, Mo!' Marwan cheered as the whole team celebrated together.

Now, what about a winner? Unfortunately, Egypt got over-excited and their inexperience cost them dearly. With seconds to go, they gave away a clumsy penalty and lost 2–1. The defeat meant that The Pharaohs wouldn't be playing at the 2012 African Cup of Nations.

'How did we throw that away?' Mohamed muttered to himself as he trudged off the pitch. International football was turning out to be a steep learning curve.

Mohamed didn't mind making mistakes – that was part of life, and part of football. What he did mind, however, was making the same mistake twice.

He couldn't let that happen, and he didn't let that happen against Niger.

Omar raced down the right and crossed to Marwan. 1–0!

Mohamed cut inside and chipped a pass to Elneny in the middle. They knew exactly what to do next. Mohamed sprinted into the box to collect the one-two and curled the ball past the goalkeeper. 2–0!

Goooooooooooooooooooooaaaaaaaaaaaaaaaaalllllllllll lllllllllllllll!!!!!!!!!!!!!!!!!!!!

What a moment – Mohamed had scored his first senior international goal! When he turned around to look for his teammates, they were there in front of him, ready to celebrate the special occasion.

'Congratulations!' Ahmed shouted. 'The first of many, I'm sure!'

Mohamed saved his biggest hug for his best friend – the other Mohamed, Mohamed Elneny. 'Thanks mate, what a pass!' he said with a massive smile on his face.

It was all looking good for Egypt ahead of their next big competition – the Under-23 African

Championships. For Mohamed Salah, it was another chance to shine. He helped his country to beat Gabon and South Africa on the way to the semi-finals.

'Come on, we can win the whole thing!' he urged his teammates.

However, after ten minutes against Morocco, Egypt were already 2–0 down. Players were crumbling under the pressure and arguing with each other, but not Mohamed. He stayed calm and composed. He knew what he needed to do.

As the cross came to him at the back post, Mohamed brought the ball down beautifully. In a flash, he curled a low shot into the bottom corner, before the goalkeeper could even react.

Goooooooooooooooooooaaaaaaaaaaaaaaaaaalllllllllllll lllllllllllll!!!!!!!!!!!!!!!!!

'I scored, and this one wasn't even a penalty!' Mohamed laughed with Ahmed.

Could they go on and complete a famous comeback? No, Morocco scored again to make it through to the final. For Egypt, it was another third-place playoff, this time against Senegal. There was still plenty to play for, though. A victory would book their place at the 2012 Olympic Games in London.

'Come on, let's get there!' Ramzy rallied his players.

Mohamed crossed for Ahmed Shroyda to score. 1–0!

Saleh Gomaa beat the keeper. 2–0!

Egypt were going to the Olympics. 'And we're going for Gold!' Ahmed announced happily.

Mohamed returned to El Mokawloon with even more confidence and purpose. He was an Egyptian international now, with exciting times ahead of him. He just needed to keep starring, keep scoring, and keep improving.

'I can do this!' Mohamed told himself.

He didn't want to be 'Egypt's *next* big thing' anymore; he was his country's present, not their future. Game by game, he was gaining the experience to go with his special talent. It was time for the next step. It was time to get consistent.

The goals soon started to flow, for club as well as country. With El Mokawloon, he scored a vicious volley against Haras El Hodood, then a brilliant one-two against Petrojet, then a long-range curler against El Gouna.

'That's three in three,' Zizo told him. He was delighted with his protégé. 'You're on fire!'

But Mohamed was just getting started. Against Ittihad El-Iskandary, his run started in the El Mokawloon half. He skipped past the first tackle and then burst between the centre-backs. In the penalty area, he took his time to place his shot past the keeper.

Goooooooooooooooooooaaaaaaaaaaaaaaaalllllllllllll lllllllllllllll!!!!!!!!!!!!!!!!!!!!

As the defenders stood there arguing with each other, Mohamed grabbed the ball and ran back for more. 'Come on!'

Against El Dakhleya, he beat the offside trap twice, like a real star striker. With his amazing sprint speed, no-one had a hope of stopping him. The first time, Mohamed shot high and the second time, he shot low. Both times, he found the net.

'Wow, what's got into you lately?' Elneny teased him. 'You can't stop scoring!'

CHAPTER 10

GOING FOR GOLD

Mohamed would never forget his first trip to London. He knew from books, films and TV shows that England's capital city was big and busy, but during the 2012 Olympics, it became even bigger and even busier. Athletes and supporters had come from all over the world for two weeks of sport and celebration.

'This place is incredible!' Mohamed gasped in amazement. Everywhere he looked, there was so much colour, noise and excitement. He felt a very long way from Nagrig now.

The Olympic football tournament was taking place all over the UK, in stadiums that Mohamed had always dreamed of playing at – Newcastle United's

St James' Park, Manchester United's Old Trafford, Wales's Millennium Stadium and, best of all, England's 'Home of Football' – Wembley Stadium.

As soon as the fixture list was available, Mohamed studied it closely. 'Come on guys, we've got to get through the group stage because I want to play at Wembley!'

Egypt had an excellent chance of doing that. After another battle against Brazil, they would face slightly easier fixtures against New Zealand and Belarus.

Mohamed watched the first half against Brazil from the bench. It was a painful but educational experience for him. Brazil's Neymar, Coutinho, Hulk and Oscar were just far too hot to handle. They ran rings around the Egypt defenders, and cruised into a 3–0 lead.

'Right now, they think we're absolute pushovers,' Hamzy told his players in the dressing room. 'They think they just have to walk out on to the pitch in the second half to win this match. Show them that isn't true – make life difficult for them!'

Hamzy's team talk worked, and so did his substitution – Mohamed on for Marwan. His shoulder was still slightly swollen but if his country needed him, then he would never say no.

Egypt quickly pulled one goal back and then went in search of another. When Elneny got the ball in midfield, he looked up and aimed for his best friend. On the edge of the penalty area, Mohamed was surrounded by three defenders but with two magical touches, he created enough space to shoot.

Goooooooooooooooooooooaaaaaaaaaaaaaaaallllllllllll llllllllllllllll!!!!!!!!!!!!!!!!!!!

It wasn't a time for celebrations. Egypt were still losing, but Mohamed was delighted to get off the mark, especially against Brazil.

'Hopefully I won't be a sub against New Zealand now!' he thought to himself.

He was right. He was in the starting line-up and he celebrated by scoring again. He stole in at the back-post to beat the keeper and rescue a point for his country. Egypt now just needed to beat Belarus to go through to the quarter-finals.

At half-time, however, it was still 0–0. What could they do to get the goal they needed? The

Pharaohs decided to use their not-so-secret weapon –
Mohamed's amazing sprint.

'Play balls over the top,' he suggested, 'and I'll run
on to them and score!'

It was a simple tactic, but Mohamed was sure that
it would work. When a pass arrived, he flicked it
forward cleverly and dribbled into the penalty area.
He used his strength to shrug off his marker and kept
the ball under close control. At the perfect moment,
he guided his shot into the bottom corner.

*Goooooooooooooooooooaaaaaaaaaaaaaaaaalllllllllll
lllllllllllll!!!!!!!!!!!!!!!!!!!*

Mohamed raced towards the corner flag with
his arms out wide. There was plenty of time for
celebrations now. He was a national hero!

'That's three goals in three games,' Ahmed said,
lifting him up on his shoulders. 'You're on fire!'

The Egypt players crouched down and kissed the
grass together. It was a joyous scene for all their
supporters, both in the stadium and back at home.

'I'm very happy that we've reached the quarter-
finals,' Mohamed told the Egyptian newspapers. He

was the man of the moment. 'It means that the team is on the right track!'

Sadly, Mohamed wouldn't get his day at Wembley. Instead, they were back at Old Trafford to take on Japan.

'We need to focus today,' Hamzy warned them before kick-off. 'They're a very good team. You have to be to beat Spain!'

Unfortunately, all of Egypt's hard work went to waste. Two sloppy mistakes left them a goal and a man down before half-time. That was a mountain that even Mohamed couldn't climb.

When he was taken off after fifty-eight minutes against Japan, Mohamed knew that Egypt's Olympics were over. There would be no medal to take home, but he was leaving London with his head held high and lots more amazing memories. With three great goals, he had proved that he belonged at the top level, alongside players like Neymar and Coutinho.

There were no tears this time. Mohamed had his next adventure to think about. He wasn't heading back to El Mokawloon. Instead, Europe was calling.

CHAPTER 11

EUROPE CALLING

Al Ahly and Zamalek had been trying to sign
Mohamed ever since his debut for El Mokawloon at
the age of sixteen. And as he improved from Egypt's
future star to Egypt's current star, the two clubs tried
even harder.

'Come join us. You'll win league titles here!'

'We can offer you everything: money, fame *and*
glory!'

It was an honour to be wanted by the top teams
in the country, but Mohamed was aiming even
higher than that. His dream was to play in Europe,
and hopefully one day in the Champions League. He
was determined to follow in the footsteps of Giggs,

Zidane, Totti and Ronaldo, those superstars that he had watched on TV as a child in Nagrig's only café.

'Never settle for second best,' Zizo advised him. 'So many talented Egyptian footballers have stayed in this country, rather than taking the next step. Fulfil your ambition, Mo! You've got everything it takes to make it big in Europe.'

Ibrahim Mahlab, the El Mokawloon Chairman, agreed. 'There's no way you're going to Al Ahly!' he argued. 'It's not about the money – it's about the talent. You're ready to play at a higher level. I believe in you!'

With the support of his club, Mohamed decided to take that brave next step. 'Okay, which European clubs want me?' he asked.

FC Basel President Bernhard Heusler had heard great things about El Mokawloon's young attacker, but he wanted to see him in action. So, he arranged a friendly match between his team and the Egypt Under-23s. Mohamed only came on in the second half, but it was worth the wait. He tore through the Swiss defence with his trickery and speed. Every time he got the ball, he was unstoppable.

'Wow, he's the fastest player I've ever seen!' Heusler thought to himself. 'We've got to sign him now, before another club swoops in.'

A month after that match, Mohamed became a Basel player for a bargain £2.25 million. He didn't know that much about his new team, but he did know the all-important information.

Basel had a growing reputation for developing young players who then went on to bigger and better things. Granit Xhaka had just signed for Borussia Mönchengladbach, while Xherdan Shaqiri had just signed for the German Champions, Bayern Munich. If he played his cards right, Mohamed might be next. On top of that, Basel had just won the Swiss title again and that meant one amazing thing:

'I'll be playing Champions League football next season!' Mohamed jumped for joy.

That thought kept him going during those first difficult months at Basel. It was a massive change, especially for a twenty-year-old who was used to quiet village life. Mohamed was on his own in a new country in a new continent, where no-one spoke his language, Arabic.

'How am I supposed to communicate with my teammates?' he moaned to his parents on the phone. 'And what am I supposed to *do?*'

Basel trained every morning but, in the afternoons and evenings, Mohamed had lots of free time. He couldn't understand any of the TV channels, so mostly he just walked around the city, feeling lonely and homesick.

'Son, don't give up,' his dad told him. 'It might not happen straight away, but you'll get used to life in Europe eventually. Remember, this is your dream!'

Mohamed thought about all those long bus journeys to Cairo and back, just to train with the El Mokawloon youth team. If he could do that, then he could do this. No, the route to the top wasn't easy, but it wasn't meant to be easy. It was a test of his character and desire, as well as his footballing skills.

'If I get to play in the Champions League,' he told himself, 'then this will all be worth it!'

Mohamed took a deep breath. He couldn't just

sit there in his hotel room, feeling sorry for himself. It was time to adapt and make the most of his extra time. He started English classes and learnt enough Swiss German phrases to understand his manager's instructions.

'That's it!' Murat Yakin clapped and cheered as he dribbled down the left wing. 'Now, get your head up for the cross!'

Mohamed also had lots to learn about Swiss football. Yes, he had the speed over twenty metres, but did he have the stamina to last the full ninety minutes? The game was played at a faster pace than in Egypt and it was more physical too. It could be very draining for a small, skilful player like him.

'Keep going, keep battling!' Yakin urged.

Mohamed did just that. He was determined to improve every aspect of his game, especially his delivery. As a winger, he would be judged on his final ball – his passes, crosses and shots. When he got his chance, he would need to get it right.

One month into the Super League season, Mohamed was selected to start for the first time against FC Thun. Wearing the Number 22 shirt, he couldn't wait to show the Basel fans what he could do.

When the ball looped up high into the air off a Thun defender, Mohamed sprinted after it, all the way into the penalty area. It felt like the good old days at El Mokawloon. Was he about to score on his Swiss league debut?

As it bounced down, he stretched his left leg towards it. Mohamed's touch took the ball round Guillaume Faivre, but the goalkeeper brought him down before he could shoot into the empty net. Penalty!

Mohamed had mixed feelings as he got back to his feet. He was pleased to win a spot-kick for his new club, but if only he had scored in the first place…

'Well done!' Basel's striker Marco Streller shouted, giving Mohamed a high-five as he scooped up the ball. 'Welcome to the team!'

CHAPTER 12

SWISS CHAMPION

Mohamed's dream debut at Basel continued. His blistering pace was just too much for FC Thun. Fifteen minutes after winning the penalty, he raced onto a long ball.

This time, Faivre was alert to the danger. He rushed out of goal and out of his penalty area altogether. But with Mohamed breathing down his neck, the keeper panicked and palmed it away with his gloves.

'Handball!' Mohamed screamed.

The referee showed Faivre a second yellow card and then a red card. Thun were down to ten men and Mohamed wasn't done yet. He helped set up Marco's second goal too, with a clever header through to David Degen. As David celebrated with Marco, he looked for Mohamed.

'Hey, come over here!' he signalled with his hand.

Mohamed smiled and jogged over to join them. He was part of the team now and he was enjoying every minute of it. He backheeled the ball to Markus Steinhöfer who in turn crossed to Marco. His header hit the bar and Valentin Stocker scored the rebound. 3–0!

The only thing missing from Mohamed's magical performance was a first Basel goal. He didn't have to wait long, however. That came a week later against FC Lausanne-Sport. When Valentin passed to him, he was in a whole island of space on the left side of the penalty area. It was 1 vs 1, attacker vs goalkeeper. Mohamed wouldn't get a better chance to score, but he had already wasted several good chances before...

This time, he held his nerve. As the keeper planted his feet and made himself as big as possible, Mohamed squeezed the ball past him.

Goooooooooooooooooooaaaaaaaaaaaaaaaalllllllllll llllllllllll!!!!!!!!!!!!!!!!

He walked towards the 30,000 fans with his

arms above his head. They stood and sang their new hero's name over and over again.

Salah! Salah! Salah!

Mohamed felt the goosebumps spreading across his skin. The feeling was even better than he was expecting. He was bursting with pride and joy.

Yet even in that incredible moment, the humble hero still knelt down to kiss the grass below his feet. Mohamed would never forget where he came from. He was lucky enough to be living his dream and he would always be thankful for that.

'They love you already!' Valentin cheered as they hugged.

Mohamed wasn't getting carried away, though, and neither was his manager. What if it was beginner's luck? What if he got injured? Yakin took Mohamed off after fifty minutes against FC St. Gallen and BSC Young Boys, and then rested him completely against FC Zürich.

'You're playing brilliantly but we really don't want you to burn out,' Yakin explained. 'I know you want to play every match but why rush? You're still only twenty! Trust me, it's my job to manage your minutes carefully and get the best out of you.'

Mohamed hated sitting on the bench, but he respected Yakin's decisions. For now, he would just have to make an impact as a super sub. How much trouble could he cause in the last thirty minutes of any match? With pace like that, the answer was lots!

For his first snowy Christmas in Switzerland, Mohamed received the perfect present. Basel's new signing was... his best friend, Mohamed Elneny! El Mokawloon's young stars were back together.

'Right, it's trophy time!' they cheered happily.

The Super League title race went right to the wire, however. Basel only won it with one game to spare. The Two Mohameds were both on the pitch when the final whistle blew.

'We did it!' they cried out. 'We're the Swiss Champions!'

They hoped that it would be the first of many trophies. Glory – that was the reason why they had swapped their beloved Egypt for Europe.

For the Champions celebration, the Two

Mohameds travelled together in a white convertible Volkswagen. They drove slowly through the city streets, happily handing out souvenir cups to the jubilant supporters, who sang:

Campiones, Campiones, Olé! Olé! Olé!

We love you Basel, we do. We love you Basel, we do.

We love you Basel, we do. Oh, Basel we love you!

The incredible night ended with music, fireworks and a captain's speech from Marco. 'Three titles in a row is amazing,' he announced proudly, 'but why not four, then five... then TEN!'

The crowd roared loudly. Mohamed Salah couldn't wait to do it all over again. His first season in Switzerland had been solid but not spectacular, with ten goals in fifty games. He knew that he could do better than that. Just as he had at El Mokawloon, he now needed to turn magical moments into magical matches. It was time to get consistent.

'You need to score more goals,' Yakin told him. 'Then you'll be a superstar.'

'Challenge accepted!' Mohamed thought to himself.

With some help from Marco, Mohamed worked extra hard on his finishing. He was happy at Basel but that didn't stop him dreaming about the big time. Perhaps one day, he would play for Real Madrid, just like Zidane and Ronaldo...

First things first, however: Mohamed needed to start firing in the Swiss Super League. In the opening match of the 2013–14 season against FC Aarau, he was determined to score. His first shot from the edge of the area landed comfortably in the goalkeeper's arms.

'What was that?!' Mohamed screamed, slapping the air. He was really annoyed at himself. It was exactly the kind of strike that he had been working on in training.

He didn't make the same mistake twice. When Valentin crossed from the left, he calmly sidefooted the ball into the back of the net.

Goooooooooooooooooooaaaaaaaaaaaaaaaalllllllllllll llllllllllllll!!!!!!!!!!!!!!!!!!!!

Twenty-three minutes played, and he was already off the mark! It was going to be a great season, Mohamed could tell.

CHAPTER 13

EUROPEAN STAR

During his first season at Basel, Mohamed only played 110 minutes of Champions League football. Just when he was finding his feet, they suffered a shock defeat to Romanian team CFR Cluj in the final qualifying round. It was a painful taster, but all was not lost. Basel would be playing in the Europa League instead.

'Maybe it's for the best,' Mohamed said, staying positive. 'This is a competition we can win!'

Basel stormed through the group stage and then past rich Russian side Zenit St Petersburg in the Round of 16. Mohamed set up the first goal and won the penalty for the second.

'Quarter-finals, here we come!' the whole team cheered together.

Mohamed was off to London again. Nine months after representing Egypt at the Olympics, he was back with Basel to take on Tottenham Hotspur. All of Europe's top teams would be watching.

In the first half at White Hart Lane, Basel found themselves 2–0 up. Marco, Mohamed and Valentin combined for the first goal, and then Fabian Frei headed home the second. The cup upset was on! Tottenham fought back to 2–2 but Basel returned to Switzerland with two important away goals.

'Spurs need to score tonight,' Yakin told his players before kick-off in St Jakob-Park. 'Do whatever it takes to stop them!'

In the twenty-third minute, however, Tottenham took the lead. Suddenly, Basel were on the back-foot, but not for long. On the counter-attack, Marco passed to Mohamed on the right wing. His first touch was heavy, but he had the speed to reach the ball first. With his second touch, he poked a shot into the bottom corner.

*Goooooooooooooooooooooaaaaaaaaaaaaaaaallllllllllll
lllllllllllll!!!!!!!!!!!!!!!!!!!!*

Mohamed turned and ran towards the Basel
bench, shaking his finger like Ronaldo at the 2002
World Cup. What a time to score his first Europa
League goal! He couldn't celebrate for long,
however. He had defending to do.

After 180 minutes of football, Basel and
Tottenham were tied at 4–4. The score-line stayed
that way, even after thirty minutes of extra-time. The
match went to penalties, but Mohamed wouldn't get
to take one. He had already been taken off.

'No, I want to be out there!' he muttered grumpily
on the sidelines.

In the end, Basel didn't need him. When Marcelo
Díaz scored their winning spot-kick, Mohamed
sprinted onto the pitch to join in the celebrations.

'Semi-finals, here we come!' the whole team
cheered together.

Mohamed was off to London again and this time,
Chelsea were the opponents. Basel were 2–1 down
from the first leg but anything could happen at

Stamford Bridge, especially with Mohamed in attack.

With seconds to go in the first half, Valentin threaded a beautiful pass through the dogged Chelsea defence. At the crucial moment, Mohamed darted between the centre-backs. When he got to the ball, he didn't even take a touch; he just lifted it over the diving goalkeeper's arms.

Goooooooooooooooooooaaaaaaaaaaaaaaaaallllllllllll llllllllllllllll!!!!!!!!!!!!!!!!!!!!!

Basel had a lifeline! Mohamed grabbed the ball and ran back for the restart. First Tottenham, now Chelsea – he was saving his best for the big games. One more goal, and Basel would be in the Europa League final.

'Come on, we can do this!' Mohamed called out.

Sadly, they couldn't. Chelsea stepped things up in the second half and won 3–1. At the final whistle, Mohamed stood with his hands on his hips and let out a big, heavy sigh. He had given everything for his team, but that still wasn't enough to win.

It took a few days for the disappointment to fade but eventually, Mohamed could see the bright side. He was one of the leading assist-makers in the competition and thanks to those two goals, he was really making a name for himself now.

Basel were back in the Champions League for the 2013–14 season. This time, Mohamed had a year of European experience behind him, and even more hunger. He led his team past Maccabi Tel Aviv and Ludogorets Razgrad, and into the group stage. He was now such a scoring machine that he barely celebrated each goal. 'Just doing my job!' he would explain with a smile and a shrug.

When he saw the other clubs in Group E, he cackled like an evil villain. Basel would face Schalke 04, Steaua Bucharest… and Chelsea.

'Yes, this is our chance for revenge!' he told his teammates.

Mohamed couldn't wait for the first fixture – Chelsea, at Stamford Bridge. The Blues scored first but that didn't dampen Basel's spirits. Mohamed was up against Ashley Cole and he was beating him every time.

As the team attacked down the left, Mohamed

stayed wide on the right. All the better for making a last-second sprint to the back-post. When the ball came to Marco in the middle, he moved it quickly on to Mohamed.

Suddenly, Mohamed was in a whole island of space again, and he had to stay calm. If not, his shot would fly high and wide. He focused on the far bottom corner and found it perfectly.

Goooooooooooooooooooooaaaaaaaaaaaaaaaalllllllllll llllllllllllll!!!!!!!!!!!!!!!!!!!

What a finish! Mohamed jumped up into Marco's arms. As he jogged back to the halfway line, he knelt down and kissed the ground. Despite the hours and hours of practice, he still felt like the luckiest man alive.

Mohamed started Basel's comeback and Marco completed it with a glancing header. 2–1 – what a result for the underdogs!

'Did you see Mourinho's face?' Marco laughed as they celebrated with the fans. 'He was fuming!'

Mohamed laughed along but he was already thinking about the rematch in Switzerland. Could

Basel do the double over Chelsea?

'Why not?' he asked himself.

With five minutes to go, the game was still goalless. Fabian Schär sent a long cross-field pass from right to left, looking for the team's brightest spark. Mohamed controlled the ball beautifully and dribbled full speed ahead, into the penalty area...

The Chelsea goalkeeper stayed on his feet for as long as he could, but eventually he had to dive. As he went down, Mohamed coolly chipped the ball over him.

Goooooooooooooooooooooaaaaaaaaaaaaaaaaalllllllllllll llllllllllllllll!!!!!!!!!!!!!!!!!!!!

Salah to the rescue! Mohamed punched the air with delight as his teammates swarmed around him. This was what being a superstar was all about – crucial goals at crucial moments in crucial games.

After the match, Heusler went into the dressing room to congratulate Basel's match-winning hero.

Mohamed shook his head modestly. 'I took seven shots today and the first six were awful. I would have stopped if it wasn't for my teammates, the coach, the fans. It was their support that got us that goal, not me.'

The club president didn't know what to say. Superstars were usually so arrogant and selfish, and yet Mohamed was humble and generous. That made him one in a million.

Despite doing the double over Chelsea, Basel finished third in Champions League Group E. They moved back to the Europa League, but not Mohamed. His time in Switzerland was over. London was calling.

CHAPTER 14

LONDON CALLING

With three goals in four games, Mohamed had really caught Mourinho's eye. His timing was perfect because the Chelsea manager was on the lookout for a new attacker to replace Juan Mata and Kevin De Bruyne. The Blues usually played with three playmakers behind a central striker. Eden Hazard was Mourinho's first choice on the left, and Oscar was his first choice in the middle. The right-wing role, however, was still up for grabs.

'That's where you come into it!' the Chelsea manager explained to Mohamed at a meeting.

Mourinho liked his wide players to be quick and hard-working, and Mohamed got big ticks in both boxes. He was also still only twenty-one and eager to develop his skills.

'You're still a raw talent,' the manager told him, 'so I can't promise that you'll play every game. But you've certainly got lots of potential!'

Mohamed understood that there was lots of competition for places at Chelsea, but wouldn't that be the case at any top team? He believed in himself and he felt ready to take on his next challenge.

Chelsea weren't the only club trying to sign him, however. Liverpool had been watching Mohamed closely for years, and they had already had an offer rejected by Basel. The Reds played really exciting attacking football, with Luis Suárez, Daniel Sturridge, Philippe Coutinho and Raheem Sterling. Was there room for a fifth fantastic forward at that kind of standard?

'Trust me, you'll have the time of your life here!' the Liverpool manager Brendan Rodgers argued.

Mohamed trusted Rodgers. He was all ready to join Liverpool, but then Mourinho got in touch. That changed everything. He had won seven league titles and two Champions League trophies.

'I can't say no to *Mourinho*, can I?' Mohamed discussed with Elneny.

'Yes, you can!' his best friend pleaded jokingly. 'Don't go to London without me!'

The bidding war began at £8 million, but there was only ever going to be one winner. Chelsea simply had more money to spend. The final price was £12 million, with an extra £4 million in add-ons.

'Congratulations, you're now the most expensive Egyptian player ever!' his brother Nasr announced excitedly. Mohamed had overtaken the former Roma striker, Mido.

Suddenly, everything happened so fast. Before he knew it, Mohamed was at Stamford Bridge, signing his contract and posing for photos with the famous blue shirt. He was Chelsea's new Number 15. The boy from Nagrig was about to become a Premier League star. It still didn't feel real.

'I'm very happy to sign for Chelsea,' Mohamed told the English media through a translator. 'I hope I can make the fans happy and have a good career here.'

This would be the second big move of his life, but Mohamed wasn't expecting it to be as difficult as the first. He was older, he was now used to European life, and plus, he wouldn't be lonely in London. He now had the love and support of his wife, Magi. They would be travelling together.

'As soon as we find somewhere to live,' Mohamed promised, 'we'll get all the Arabic TV channels!'

It didn't take long for their balloon to burst. Living in London was very different to living in Basel. The city was so big, so busy and so bustling. It was overwhelming for any newcomer, but especially for a quiet kid from a small village in Egypt.

'Sometimes, I just want some peace and quiet!' Mohamed complained to Magi.

And playing for Chelsea was very different to playing for Basel. Basel was the biggest club in Switzerland, but compared to Chelsea, it was like a friendly local team.

Stamford Bridge, therefore, was a brave new world for Mohamed. The Chelsea dressing room was full of big, loud characters with lots of confidence. It was a daunting place for someone like Mohamed, who was humble and shy.

Where would he fit in? Arriving in the middle of the season was particularly hard. One day he was having a laugh with Marco, Elneny and Valentin, and the next he was sharing a football pitch with international superstars like John Terry, Frank Lampard and Fernando Torres.

'You should see those guys in training,' Mohamed told Elneny on the phone. 'Every touch is absolutely perfect. They're *so* professional!'

And strong. He had lots to learn. Mohamed hadn't realised just how intense and physical English football was. Unless he upped his game, powerful defenders like Terry, Gary Cahill and Branislav Ivanović would destroy him before he even got the ball.

'If that's what it's like in practice,' Mohamed said, 'what's it going to be like in a real match?'

He soon found out. With Chelsea beating Newcastle United 3–0, Mourinho brought Mohamed on for the last fifteen minutes.

'Good luck!' his Brazilian teammate Willian told Mohamed as he came off.

Mohamed jogged onto the field and took up a position on the right wing. He might not get many chances at Chelsea, so he had to make the most of this one.

His first touch was a simple one-two with Frank. So far, so good. But when Frank passed it straight back, Mohamed let the ball slip under his foot. He immediately chased after the Newcastle midfielder, trying to make up for his basic mistake.

'Come on, you're better than that!' he told himself.

As André Schürrle dribbled forward on the counter-attack, Mohamed burst through the middle, pointing for the pass. What an opportunity to grab a debut goal! As the ball rolled towards him, he struck it first time, and totally fluffed it. Mohamed's first shot for Chelsea rolled well wide of the target.

'Sorry!' he signalled to André, who had kept running for the return pass.

Two minutes later, Mohamed got a second

chance. Oscar stole the ball and again, Mohamed burst through the middle, pointing for the pass. This time, he took the time to steady himself before shooting. The only problem was that it was on his weaker right foot. Despite all the practice, it still wasn't as lethal as his left.

'Shoot!' the Chelsea fans urged.

Mohamed didn't feel confident and he didn't look confident either. His strike was tame, and the Newcastle goalkeeper made an easy save.

'Rubbish!' the Chelsea fans groaned.

Mohamed swatted at the air and hung his head in shame. How many more chances would he get at Chelsea?

CHAPTER 15

WORLD CUP DREAM – PART I

When Egypt missed out on the 2010 World Cup, Mohamed was still only a promising teenager. He hadn't even made his international debut yet. Four years on, however, and he was one of the most exciting young players in European club football. Could Mohamed lead his country to glory?

Although Egypt had failed to qualify for the African Cup of Nations for the second year in a row, there were hopeful signs. The Under-23s had performed well at the 2012 Olympics in London and they now formed the core of the national team – Ahmed Hegazi in defence, Elneny in midfield and Mohamed in attack.

'Let's do this!' the trio cheered together. They

were best friends on and off the pitch.

In his dreams, Mohamed had always pictured himself playing at the 2018 World Cup. He would be in his mid-twenties by then, with lots of experience for club and country. But why not 2014 as well?

'There's no reason why we can't make it to Brazil!' Egypt's manager Bob Bradley told his players. He knew what he was talking about; he had coached the USA national team at the 2010 World Cup in South Africa.

Egypt started the qualifying campaign in style, winning six games out of six. Mohamed was their top scorer with six goals, including his first-ever hat-trick against Zimbabwe. All three were fantastic finishes but the second was the pick of the bunch.

Mohamed dribbled all the way from the halfway line, nutmegged one defender and then sprinted towards the penalty area. After hurdling a last-ditch tackle, he chipped the ball cheekily over the diving keeper.

Gooooooooooooooaaaaaaaaaalllllllllllllllllllllllll!!!!!!!!!!!

Mohamed was head and shoulders above his opponents, just like when he used to play on the local pitch in Nagrig. If he didn't actually score a goal for Egypt, he would usually set it up with a clever cross or pass. He was involved in everything.

'What would we do without you?' Ahmed asked but no-one wanted to think about that awful possibility.

Thanks to Mohamed, Egypt finished top of Group G. They were now just two games away from a place at the 2014 World Cup. They would be two very difficult matches, however, against Ghana. The Black Stars were one of the best teams in Africa. They had great players like Michael Essien and Asamoah Gyan, and they had reached the quarter-finals of the 2010 World Cup.

'If we defend well in Ghana, then we'll beat them back in Cairo!' Bradley said to motivate his team.

Unfortunately, Gyan scored Ghana's first goal in the fourth minute. After that, it quickly became a humiliation for Egypt – without Ahmed at the back, the Egypt backline collapsed. They scored a clumsy own goal and then gave away a silly penalty.

'No, no, NO!'

Mohamed couldn't believe what he was seeing. The team had played so well up until now, so why were they suddenly making every mistake under the sun? Mohamed did his best to turn things around. He won a penalty at the end of the first half, but that was little comfort. Egypt lost 6–1, leaving their World Cup hopes in ruins.

As they returned to the dressing room, Egypt's players were speechless with shock and shame. They knew Ghana were a very good team, but they still felt they had let their country down.

'Look guys, all we can do is stay strong and win the second leg in Cairo,' their captain Mohamed Aboutrika said to break the silence.

Egypt won that second leg 2–1 but that was nowhere near enough. There would be no World Cup adventure for The Pharaohs, not this time.

'Well played,' Mohamed Salah said, shaking hands with Essien and Gyan at full-time.

He was very disappointed, but it was no time for despair. Instead, the Egypt players needed to use the painful experience to spur them on. They were improving, and this was just a setback on the road to success.

'2018,' Mohamed kept saying, '2018 will be *ours!*'

Mohamed watched the 2014 tournament on TV, wishing and learning. He paid close attention to Messi and Neymar, and the World Cup's breakout star, James Rodríguez of Colombia. If he kept working hard, that could be Mohamed in four years' time.

Nigeria and Algeria made it as far as the second round, but there wasn't a single African nation in the quarter-finals. Mohamed was determined to change that.

'When we qualify in 2018,' he told Ahmed and Elneny, 'we have to at least get through our group, okay?'

'Okay!' they promised.

Mohamed was living out his dreams, one by one:

Become a professional footballer – tick!

Play for his country – tick!

Move to Europe – tick!

Win a league title – tick!

Play in the Champions League, just like his childhood heroes – tick!

Play at a World Cup – not yet, but that was next on Mohamed's list.

CHAPTER 16

CHANCES AT CHELSEA

After those fifteen minutes against Newcastle, Mohamed got just five against West Brom, then zero against Everton. Against Fulham, he wasn't on the bench at all.

'What did I do wrong?' Mohamed wanted to ask.

He felt like he was going backwards, not forwards. He had never played so little football, not even during his early days at Basel. Mohamed wasn't sixteen years old anymore; he was twenty-one!

'I know Mourinho warned me to be patient,' he told his brother, 'but how long do I have to wait? Weeks? Months? Years?'

Nasr didn't have the answer. 'Until he thinks

you're ready, I guess.'

Mohamed could be waiting forever, especially with André Schürrle playing so well on the right. And if André had a bad game, Mourinho could bring on Willian, or Ramires, or Demba Ba instead. Chelsea had so many attacking options to choose from.

'You'll get another chance soon,' Eden Hazard reassured Mohamed.

In the London derby against Arsenal, The Blues were 4–0 up by half-time. As each goal went in, Mohamed's legs grew more and more restless on the subs bench. He wanted to be out there, joining in the fun. After sixty-five minutes, Mohamed got his wish. Could he add his name to the scoresheet? He would certainly give it his best shot.

The Arsenal defenders were already suffering; the last thing they wanted was an opponent with Mohamed's amazing sprint speed. As Nemanja Matić chipped a pass over the top, he was already on the run.

'Offside!' the defenders hoped but the linesman's flag stayed down.

Mohamed was through, one on one with

the goalkeeper. Oh boy, this was it – his huge goalscoring chance! This time, he kept calm and slid the ball under the keeper's diving body.

Goooooooooooooaaaaaaaaaallllllllllllllllllllll!!!!!!!!!!!

Mohamed had never felt such relief in all his life. It had finally arrived – his first Chelsea goal. He knelt down and kissed the ground. He had so much to be thankful for.

What next? Chelsea were through to the quarter-finals of the Champions League. Mohamed was still cup-tied but hopefully, he would now get more Premier League game-time.

Against Stoke City, Mourinho rested both Eden and Oscar. Mohamed got his hopes up and this time, he wasn't disappointed. His name and number were there on the teamsheet – '15 SALAH'! Mohamed was about to make his first league start for Chelsea.

'Bring it on!' he thought to himself. He was so excited that he nearly shouted it out loud.

Mohamed knew what he needed to do, and he knew that he could do it. He just needed to think less and believe more. He had earned this opportunity.

After thirty minutes, Nemanja dribbled down the left wing and muscled his way into the box. As he looked to cut the ball back, the Chelsea midfielder had two targets near the penalty spot – Willian and Mohamed. He picked Mohamed.

The ball was coming towards him at speed, so Mohamed didn't have time to think. That was probably a good thing. He had to rely on his natural instinct instead.

Mohamed struck the ball sweetly and it flew through the crowd of players and towards the bottom corner. The Stoke goalkeeper reached it but he couldn't keep it out.

Goooooooooooooaaaaaaaaaallllllllllllllllllllll!!!!!!!!!!!

Mohamed ran straight over to Nemanja to thank him for the assist. Then he knelt down to kiss the ground as usual. As he stood up again, Mohamed came face-to-face with Frank Lampard, who gave him a high-five and a hug.

'Great finish, Mo!' he cheered.

Frank's praise meant the world to him. Finally, he was finding his feet at Chelsea. Mohamed won the penalty for the second goal and set up Willian's third too.

'Surely Mourinho can't drop you now!' his brother told him on the phone. In Egypt, Nasr watched every game.

Mohamed wasn't so sure. There was so much competition for places. One poor performance, and he could find himself back on the bench. He had to keep up the good work.

In Chelsea's next match against Swansea, Mohamed played well but he wasted a few key chances to score. Once, he hit the post and another time, he fired wide. Would those misses come back to haunt him?

He always remembered his old Basel manager's words – 'You need to score more goals. Then, you'll be a superstar.'

Mohamed wanted to be a superstar so much. He played in all of Chelsea's last four league matches but there were no more goals and no more assists either.

In each game, Mourinho took him off slightly earlier: the sixty-sixth minute against Sunderland, then the sixtieth minute against Liverpool, then at half-time against Norwich.

Had Mohamed blown his chances at Chelsea? He could feel his confidence fading away with each failed shot at goal.

'Just relax!' his dad advised him. 'You're putting too much pressure on yourself.'

Relax? Mohamed didn't know the meaning of the word. Football was his life; it meant everything to him. He spent the summer getting stronger and sharper. He wasn't giving up without a fight.

'Last season was just my warm-up,' he told himself. 'Now, it's time to show Mourinho what I'm really made of!'

Mohamed scored a few goals in preseason but when the 2014-15 Premier League campaign kicked off, Chelsea forgot about him.

'I just want to play regular football,' he admitted to his wife Magi. Perhaps Mohamed needed a change of scene to rediscover his top form.

CHAPTER 17

FIRING AGAIN AT FIORENTINA

Chelsea sent their talented young players out on loan to clubs all over Europe. Christian Atsu was at Everton, Bertrand Traoré was at Vitesse Arnhem in the Netherlands, and Lucas Piazon was at Eintracht Frankfurt in Germany. It was the best way for them to gain lots of first-team experience.

Chelsea's scouts watched every game and then reported back to Mourinho. If someone was playing really well, the manager might then bring them back to Stamford Bridge.

'It beats playing for the Reserves!' Marco van Ginkel argued. He was enjoying his time at AC Milan in Italy.

Mohamed really didn't want to leave Chelsea, but it seemed like the only way to rediscover his confidence and form. When the January 2015 transfer window opened, he had only played in nine matches and he hadn't scored a single goal. His Premier League dream really wasn't working out, but he couldn't just sit around hoping for things to change. It was time to take his career into his own hands.

'I need to start playing more football again,' Mohamed told Mourinho. 'Let me go somewhere on loan for six months and then I'll come back better than ever!'

The Chelsea manager was impressed by his young player's hunger. 'I think that's a good idea,' he agreed. 'Leave it with me – I'll find a good club for you.'

When Colombian winger Juan Cuadrado moved from Fiorentina to Chelsea, Mohamed moved in the opposite direction. This was the fresh start Mohamed needed. He chose the Number 74 shirt, in memory of the seventy-four Egyptian football fans who had tragically died in the Port Said Stadium riot.

Mohamed was looking forward to his Italian adventure. 'The Viola' were sixth in Serie A and they were still in the Europa League too.

'Welcome!' the Fiorentina manager Vincenzo Montella said, shaking Mohamed's hand. 'You've got big boots to fill.'

Montella was referring to Cuadrado, who had been the team's creative star, scoring great goals and setting up lots more for strikers Mario Gómez and Khouma Babacar.

But Mohamed replied with great confidence: 'Don't worry, I can fill them!' All he needed was a chance and the support of his manager.

Montella thought that his new signing would need time to adapt to Italian football, but he thought wrong. On his full debut against Sassuolo, Mohamed chased after Khouma's clever flick-on. With his amazing sprint speed, he raced away from the defenders. In a flash, he was into the penalty area, with just the goalkeeper to beat...

Mohamed knew that he needed to finish it calmly

and carefully. He wasn't going to waste another chance to score. He guided his shot straight into the bottom corner.

Goooooooooooooooooooooaaaaaaaaaaaaaaaaalllllllllllll llllllllllllllll!!!!!!!!!!!!!!!!!!!!

He was off the mark! Mohamed jogged over to the Fiorentina fans behind the goal and raised his arms aloft. It felt fantastic to be back on the scoresheet so quickly. When he set up the second goal for Khouma, Khouma joked, 'Cuadrado who? We don't need him now that we've got you!'

Mohamed was a man on a mission. Now that he had one goal under his belt, he wanted lots more. He was like a busy bee, buzzing around the box. Suddenly, he couldn't stop scoring.

He scored with his right foot against Torino, then with his left foot against Inter Milan. Against Sampdoria, he weaved his way past two defenders before shooting past the keeper. Against Empoli, he held off two defenders, tricked them with a beautiful turn, and still found the back of the net.

'I knew you were good,' Alberto Aquilani cheered

over the noise of the Fiorentina fans, 'but I didn't know you were *this* good!'

Mohamed had always known, and he had always believed in his talent. Finally, the rest of the world was starting to believe too. He just hoped that Mourinho was watching.

It was hard to miss Mohamed's red-hot form. In the Europa League, he tore the Tottenham defence apart again, with his speed and determination. Jan Vertonghen thought he could shepherd the ball back to his goalkeeper, but not with Mohamed around.

Gooooooooooooooooooooaaaaaaaaaaaaaaaalllllllllllll llllllllllllll!!!!!!!!!!!!!!!!!!!

He was having the time of his life in Italy, and he was already the fans' favourite. Fiorentina didn't win any trophies, but they finished fourth in Serie A and got to the semi-finals of both the Europa League and the Coppa Italia.

In the first leg against Juventus in the Coppa Italia, Mohamed played perhaps his best game in the purple shirt. After ten minutes, a Fiorentina clearance fell to him inside his own half. Mohamed was on his own, with two defenders chasing him and one coming towards him. Fortunately, his confidence was sky-high, and his sprint speed was second to none. *Nutmeg!* Mohamed raced through into the penalty area and blasted the ball into the net.

Goooooooooooooooooooooaaaaaaaaaaaaaaaaaallllllllllllll llllllllllllllll!!!!!!!!!!!!!!!!!!!!!

What a wondergoal! Mohamed jogged over to the corner, pointing up at the sky. Then he knelt down and kissed the ground. Even when he was on top of the world, he still stayed humble.

It took a while for Mohamed's teammates to catch up with him.

'Have you got a motor hidden in your boots or something?' Mario joked as he hugged the hero. 'I've never seen anyone run that fast!'

In the second half, Mohamed was at it again. He got the ball and glided through the Juventus defence, before stroking the ball into the bottom corner with ease. Now he had truly found his composure that had been missing at Chelsea.

The Fiorentina fans did not want to lose Mohamed

at the end of the season. 'Mo, please don't go!'
they begged. What would they do without their
new star player?

Mohamed was in no hurry to return to England.
It had been a real season of two halves for him.
After his frustrations at Chelsea, he had found a new
lease of life on loan at Fiorentina, scoring nine goals
in twenty-nine games. It was the best decision he
had ever made. The Italian club had made him feel
welcome and wanted.

The big question now was would Chelsea want
Mohamed back at Stamford Bridge?

CHAPTER 18

ROARING AT ROMA

The answer was no; Chelsea didn't want Mohamed back at Stamford Bridge. Not yet, anyway. He didn't go to the USA on the club's preseason tour, and Mourinho signed a new right winger to replace him – Pedro from Barcelona.

'I want to go out on loan again,' Mohamed told his manager firmly. 'I'm twenty-three years old now, and I *have* to play football!'

Fiorentina were desperate to have him back, but it wasn't a one-club race anymore. Roma had just finished second in Serie A and they were looking to strengthen their attack. They saw Mohamed as the perfect signing. He had lots of speed and skill, and he had already shown that he could score goals in Italy.

Sadly, Fiorentina didn't have the money to rival Roma, or the ambition.

'Our aim is to win the league this year,' Roma's president James Pallotta explained to Mohamed, 'and we want to go far in the Champions League too. You're exactly the exciting attacker we need!'

Mohamed was impressed. At Roma, not only would he get the chance to play Champions League football again, but he would also get the chance to play Champions League football with Francesco Totti, his childhood hero.

'Let's do this!' Mohamed decided.

He arrived in Italy's capital city on a one-year loan but if all went well, Roma would be able to sign him permanently for £13 million.

'Let's wait and see!' Mohamed thought to himself. For now, he just wanted to play well and score goals.

His first goal for his new club was an absolute cracker. Roma were losing 2–1 to Sassuolo when a corner-kick was headed out to the edge of the area. As it dropped towards him, Mohamed had a decision to make. He didn't take many long-range shots; he scored most of his goals in the penalty areas, in one-on-ones with the keeper.

But what was the worst that could happen? He didn't mind making a fool of himself, by slicing it wide or missing the ball completely. If he didn't try, how could he ever succeed? He had his confidence back, and he had new fans to impress.

Mohamed watched the ball carefully and struck it sweetly on the volley with his lethal left foot. It swerved through the air, past a crowd of players, and then dipped down into the bottom corner.

Gooooooooooooooooooooaaaaaaaaaaaaaaaaalllllllllllll llllllllllllllll!!!!!!!!!!!!!!!!!!!

Mohamed fell to his knees and kissed the ground. What a way to start his Roma career! The 30,000 fans in the Stadio Olimpico went absolutely wild, waving their scarves above their heads. They showed such passion for the club and Mohamed was their new hero. As he got back to his feet, he came face to face with Francesco Totti, who gave him a hug.

'What a strike, Mo!' he cheered.

The Roma legend's praise meant the world to him. After all, when he was a kid, Mohamed had dreamed of being able to shoot like Totti.

At the end of October, it was time for Mohamed to return to Fiorentina. It turned out to be a very dramatic return indeed. In the seventh minute, he gave Roma the lead with a curling left-foot shot. 1–0!

As his teammates ran over to celebrate with him, Mohamed raised his arms and shook his head. No, he wanted to show respect to the Fiorentina fans who had always shown him so much love and support. He was ever the humble hero.

With five minutes to go, Roma were heading for a comfortable 2–0 victory in Florence. Mohamed was usually so calm on the football pitch, but for the first time ever, he lost his temper for a second. As he battled for the ball with Facundo Roncaglia, he kicked the defender's ankle. *Free-kick!* The referee blew the whistle and rushed over to show Mohamed a yellow card.

'Whatever!' he responded, waving an arm in the air.

As he ran back into position, Mohamed heard the whistle again. He turned around, and he couldn't believe his eyes. The referee was showing him a second yellow, and then a red card!

In all his years of football, Mohamed had never been sent off before. The decision was so shocking that he could only laugh as he walked off the pitch. 'A yellow card for waving my arm?' he thought to himself. 'That's the stupidest thing ever!'

That sending-off was the only setback in another very successful Italian season for Mohamed. After a decent start, his form got even better once Luciano Spalletti became the new Roma manager. Spalletti was his favourite kind of coach. He was always looking to make his players feel good and help them to improve.

Mohamed asked the question that he asked every manager – 'What do I need to do to reach the next level?'

'You're one of the most talented players I've ever worked with,' Spalletti replied. 'In terms of tactics, however, I think there are ways that you could improve.'

Mohamed was still as eager as ever to learn new skills. With his manager's help, he became a much smarter footballer. He learnt when to defend and when to attack, when to drop deep and when to burst into the box, when to shoot and when to pass.

'Superstars make the right decision almost every time,' Spalletti explained. 'They're always one step ahead of the game.'

Mohamed scored two goals against Palermo, and two more against his old team Fiorentina. He also set up Edin Džeko's opening goal against Udinese, and Radja Nainggolan's winner against Napoli.

At the San Siro, Mohamed dribbled into the AC Milan penalty area. The Roma fans were up on their feet, ready to celebrate, but he dragged his shot wide. They couldn't believe it, and neither could he.

'What was that?' Mohamed screamed, looking up at the sky for an answer.

During his difficult days at Chelsea, his head would have dropped after a miss like that. Not anymore, though. Mohamed was now a totally different player – older, wiser and a whole lot better.

A few minutes later, he dribbled into the AC Milan penalty area again and he didn't make the same mistake twice.

Goooooooooooooooooooaaaaaaaaaaaaaaaaalllllllllllll llllllllllllll!!!!!!!!!!!!!!!!!!

It was the perfect way for Mohamed to end his best-ever season. Chelsea's loss had been Roma's gain. With fifteen goals in forty-two games, he was the team's top scorer and their Player of the Year.

'What a bargain!' Pallotta cheered as Roma signed Mohamed for £13 million.

CHAPTER 19

AFRICAN CUP OF NATIONS

In 2017, Egypt finally qualified for their first African Cup of Nations since Mohamed's international debut.

'Fourth time lucky!' he joked with Ahmed and Elneny.

There was nothing lucky about it, however. Egypt cruised through qualification, beating Tanzania, Chad and even the favourites, Nigeria. Mohamed was their top scorer with four goals, but it was a real team effort.

The Pharaohs were getting better and better. There were now lots of Egyptians playing all over Europe – in Greece, Belgium, Portugal and France.

Omar Gaber was at Mohamed's old club Basel, while Elneny had moved to London to play for Arsenal.

'It's time to show the world what you can do together!' their new manager, Héctor Cúper, told them as they arrived in Gabon for the big tournament.

Mohamed couldn't wait to get started. The 2018 World Cup was only eighteen months away and this was the perfect chance for Egypt to build up their confidence and togetherness. In Group D, they faced Mali, Uganda, and Ghana, the team that had knocked them out in the qualification for the 2014 World Cup. Were Egypt ready for revenge?

It didn't look like it in their first game when they drew 0–0 with Mali. And The Pharaohs were heading for another 0–0 draw against Uganda, until the eighty-ninth minute. Mohamed was having a quiet match but suddenly, he sprang to life. As Egypt attacked, he sprinted through the middle, calling out, 'Pass!'

Mohamed's first touch was heavy, but he had the speed to reach the ball first. What next? He was inside the penalty area, on his lethal left foot.

However, he was off-balance, and a defender was blocking his path to goal.

Mohamed remembered Spalletti's message: 'Superstars make the right decision almost every time. They're always one step ahead of the game.'

So, what was the right decision? Out of the corner of his eye, he saw Abdallah El Said rushing forward on his right. Mohamed faked to shoot and passed across to Abdallah, who nutmegged the keeper.

Goooooooooooooooooooooaaaaaaaaaaaaaaaaalllllllllllll lllllllllllllllll!!!!!!!!!!!!!!!!!!!

The Egypt fans jumped for joy and so did all the players. What an important moment for their nation! Abdallah was the goalscoring hero, but it was Mohamed's awareness that had saved the day.

'You're a genius!' Elneny cried out as they hugged.

Mohamed shrugged modestly, but that assist changed everything. It brought so much confidence to the team, just in time for their rematch with Ghana.

'Bring it on!' they cheered.

At Roma, Francesco was usually the first choice

to take free kicks, then Edin, then Radja. Mohamed hardly ever took them. For Egypt, however, he had more responsibility. He was the one the others turned to when they needed a moment of magic.

In the eleventh minute against Ghana, The Pharaohs won a free kick in the middle of the pitch, just outside the penalty area. Mohamed placed the ball down, stepped back and looked up at the target.

'I can do this,' he told himself.

Mohamed had been practising for weeks, and his country was counting on him. When the referee blew the whistle, he ran up and struck the ball with power and accuracy. It flew straight as an arrow into the top corner.

Goooooooooooooooooooooaaaaaaaaaaaaaaaaalllllllllllll llllllllllllll!!!!!!!!!!!!!!!!!!!

Mohamed barely celebrated as his teammates piled on top of him. The smile on his face was the only sign that something special had just happened.

That free kick turned out to be the matchwinner. After a poor start for Egypt, Mohamed had taken them to the top of Group D, and into the quarter-finals. With a third 1–0 victory in a row, they battled their way past Morocco too.

'We never give up!' Mohamed cheered at the final whistle. He was so proud of all his teammates.

In the semi-finals, Egypt took on the tournament's other surprise package, Burkina Faso. 'The Stallions' had drawn with Cameroon before beating Tunisia.

'This is going to be our toughest game yet,' Cúper warned his players. 'Don't underestimate them. There's no room for mistakes!'

Egypt took the lead in the second half, and it was Mohamed to the rescue again. From the edge of the box, he curled another incredible shot into the top corner.

Goooooooooooooooooooooaaaaaaaaaaaaaaaalllllllllllll llllllllllllll!!!!!!!!!!!!!!!!!!!

Mohamed was having the best tournament of his career, even better than the 2012 Olympics in London. He was living up to all expectations.

'What a strike!' Ahmed cheered as the whole team hugged their hero.

Burkina Faso scored a great goal of their own,

however, and the semi-final went to extra-time and then penalties. This time, Mohamed was still on the pitch. 'I'll take one,' he said straight away.

Abdallah went first for Egypt, but he hit the post! It was the worst start possible, but The Pharaohs never stopped believing. Ramadan Sobhi scored and so did Ahmed. It wasn't over yet.

As Mohamed made the long walk to the penalty spot, he looked as calm as ever. Pressure, what pressure? He placed the ball down, stepped back and looked up at the target.

'I can do this,' he told himself.

The Burkina Faso goalkeeper guessed the right way, but Mohamed's shot was just too good.

Gooooooooooooooooooooaaaaaaaaaaaaaaaallllllllllll llllllllllllll!!!!!!!!!!!!!!!!!

As he walked back to the halfway line, he looked over at his goalkeeper, Essam El-Hadary, as if to say, 'It's your turn to be our hero now.'

Essam didn't let Egypt down. With two brilliant spot-kick saves, he took them into the African Cup of Nations final!

Mohamed used his amazing sprint speed to reach his goalkeeper first. 'What a hero!' he cried out. 'I knew we could do it!'

In the final, Egypt were up against the mighty Cameroon. 'The Indomitable Lions' had already beaten Senegal and Ghana. Were they going to gobble up Egypt too?

'We have to be fearless today,' Essam told his teammates before they walked out onto the pitch. 'We're the best team in Africa!'

Egypt started the game brilliantly. Mohamed dribbled in off the right wing and slipped a great pass through to Elneny, who kept his cool and fooled the goalkeeper. 1–0!

'Where did you learn to shoot like that?' Mohamed teased his friend. 'It must have been me!'

Could The Pharaohs hold on to their lead this time? No, Cameroon equalised after sixty minutes, and the last half hour was unbearably tense. Who would get the winning goal? Egypt looked to Mohamed, but the long balls weren't reaching him.

Just when it looked like the final would go to

extra-time, Cameroon scored. As he watched Vincent Aboubakar's shot hit the back of the net, Mohamed's heart sank. It felt like someone had kicked him in the guts. It wasn't time to despair just yet, though. He still had five minutes to try and save the day.

'Come on!' Mohamed roared.

As hard as he tried, however, he couldn't find a way through the Cameroon defence. At the final whistle, the Egypt players fell to the floor, exhausted and defeated.

'I know it hurts but you should be so proud of yourselves,' Cúper said, trying to lift their spirits. 'You've come so far. We didn't even qualify last time!'

At first, nothing could make Mohamed feel better, not even being named in the Team of the Tournament. After a few miserable days, however, he moved on. He had to if he wanted to achieve his next aims – World Cup qualification with Egypt and the Serie A title with Roma.

CHAPTER 20

MOHAMED AND EDIN

Mohamed had waved goodbye to Chelsea for good. He was now a permanent Roma player, and so was Edin. They had already formed a strong partnership in attack, but it was time to take that to the next level.

'Let's become Italy's deadliest duo!' they decided.

They made a perfect pair. Mohamed had speed and skill, while Edin had height and power. Most importantly, they shared two great passions – scoring and winning.

In Roma's first match of the new season against Udinese, Edin won the first penalty, and Mohamed won the second. 2–0! Edin scored the third goal, and

Mohamed scored the fourth. 4–0!

'I've got a very good feeling about this season!' their teammate Radja said with a smile.

Mohamed had a very good feeling too. He was off to a great start and, playing week in week out, he could feel himself getting better and better.

There was a lot more to Mohamed's game than just scoring goals – much more! He was a real team player. Spalletti asked his star right winger to defend from the front and create chances for Edin. Away at Napoli, he showed both skills in one amazing move.

As Kalidou Koulibaly tried to let the ball roll out for a goal kick, Mohamed chased him all the way. Using his strength, he blocked the big defender's clearance and played a great cross to Edin. 1–0 to Roma! Edin ran straight over to hug and thank his strike partner.

'No problem,' Mohamed replied. 'Just doing my job!'

He wasn't just doing his job, though; he was doing his job *brilliantly*. Mohamed was helping to keep Roma right behind Juventus at the top of the table.

'Come on, we can win the league this season!'

Spalletti clapped and cheered on the sidelines.

Roma hadn't won the Italian title for fifteen years, but with Mohamed and Edin up front, anything felt possible. They were the deadliest duo around, and a defender's worst nightmare.

'Chelsea must be really kicking themselves!' Mohamed's dad laughed. 'How could they let you leave for £13 million?'

By the Christmas break, Mohamed and Edin had already scored twenty-one goals between them, and that was only in Serie A. They were on fire in other competitions too.

In the Europa League against Villarreal, Mohamed raced down the right wing. He hardly needed to look up because he knew exactly where Edin would be. *GOAL!*

Against Lyon, Edin returned the favour. With a cheeky flick, he fooled the defender and set Mohamed away. He sprinted into the penalty area and coolly nutmegged the keeper.

Goooooooooooooooooooooaaaaaaaaaaaaaaaaaalllllllllllll llllllllllllll!!!!!!!!!!!!!!!!!!!

In the semi-finals of the Coppa Italia, Roma were losing 4–1 to their local rivals, Lazio. It was a total disaster. Some of their fans had given up hope, but not Mohamed. He still believed.

When Stephan El Shaarawy's shot hit the post, he pounced to score the rebound. 4–2!

When the keeper parried Radja's fierce strike, he was in the right place at the right time again. 4–3!

'Hey, stop stealing my goals!' Edin joked.

Mohamed shrugged modestly and smiled. It was all part of his special superstar training.

'Superstars make the right decision almost every time,' Spalletti kept telling him. 'They're always one step ahead of the game.'

Mohamed wasn't quite a superstar yet, but it was only a matter of practice and game-time. His decision-making was improving with every match. He finished the season with a terrific total of nineteen goals and twelve assists.

'Congratulations, all that hard work is really paying off!' his manager praised him.

In terms of silverware, however, Mohamed ended

up empty-handed yet again. Roma were runners-up behind Juventus in Serie A, and they got knocked out of the Europa League and the Coppa Italia. Mohamed's trophy cabinet was still bare, except for one Swiss Super League title at Basel.

Mohamed was hungry for more; much more. He had made the big, bold move from Egypt to Europe in order to win the top football trophies – the English Premier League, the Italian League, the Europa League, the Champions League – and that was what he was going to do, no matter what.

Mohamed wanted to win the top football trophies with Roma. But if they couldn't, he would just have to find another club that could.

CHAPTER 21

WORLD CUP DREAM – PART II

'Mo, you're our penalty taker now,' Mahmoud Fayez, the Egypt assistant manager, said one day as the squad prepared for the 2018 World Cup qualifiers.

Mohamed nodded calmly and carried on as normal. It was no big deal. He was used to handling high-pressure situations, especially for his national team. He was already Egypt's star player, so what difference would one extra responsibility make? Mohamed had scored from the spot in the 2017 African Cup of Nations semi-final against Burkina Faso. He could do it again if his country needed him.

Egypt hadn't played at a World Cup since 1990.

As the years had gone by, it was becoming more and more embarrassing. When would The Pharaohs finally get back to where they belonged, in football's greatest tournament?

Hopes were sky-high for Egypt in 2018. They had come so close to qualifying for 2014 and four years on, their best players were even better. Ahmed was now playing for West Brom, Elneny was at Arsenal, and Mohamed was on fire at Roma.

'This is *our* time,' the fans declared confidently.

The players shared their belief. Mohamed wasn't going to watch another World Cup at home on TV; he couldn't bear it. This time, he was going to make sure he would be there, playing for his country.

To qualify, Egypt needed to top Group E, above Congo, Uganda and their old rivals, Ghana. 'No problem!' they thought to themselves but after forty minutes against Congo, they were 1–0 down.

'Come on, wake up!' Mohamed shouted.

Usually, he didn't say much out on the pitch; he let his lethal left foot do the talking instead. But when Mohamed did speak, everyone listened carefully.

Suddenly, Egypt sprang to life. As the cross came in from the left, Mohamed watched it closely, like a predator watching its prey. Thanks to the lessons he had learned from Spalletti and Edin at Roma, he knew exactly what to do next. He stepped away from his marker, jumped up high, and angled his header down into the far corner of the net.

Goooooooooooooooooooaaaaaaaaaaaaaaaaalllllllllllll lllllllllllllll!!!!!!!!!!!!!!!!!!!!

Mohamed to the rescue: 1–1! He was delighted. Not only was it a rare header, but it was an absolute beauty.

'Thanks, mate!' Elneny cheered. 'We really needed that!'

'Thank Abdelshafy,' he replied modestly. 'That cross was awesome!'

In the second half, Mohamed chased onto a long ball and laid it back for Abdallah Said to strike. 2–1 to Egypt!

Two key moments – two key decisions. Mohamed was becoming a real superstar. The whole squad celebrated together, including the substitutes. It meant so much to all of them because they shared the same dream.

'World Cup 2018, here we come!'

Next up: Ghana. Mohamed knew that it would be a tight match with few goalscoring chances. Egypt would need their big game players.

With half-time approaching, Trezeguet dribbled into the Ghana box. As he burst through, a defender lunged in with a clumsy tackle.

'Penalty!' the Egypt players cried out and the referee pointed to the spot.

Mohamed pulled up his socks and took a deep breath. What a massive moment! The whole nation was counting on him. If he scored, he would be Egypt's hero, leading them one step closer to the 2018 World Cup. But if he missed – no, he didn't even want to think about that possibility. Mohamed ran up and sent the keeper the wrong way.

Goooooooooooooooooooooaaaaaaaaaaaaaaaaalllllllllllll lllllllllllllll!!!!!!!!!!!!!!!!!!!

As the relief rushed through his body, Mohamed threw his arms out wide and then blew a kiss to his beloved country. The Egyptian people had never doubted him for a second.

'Yes, Mo, you did it!' Elneny shouted over and over again until his throat got sore.

Two wins out of two put Egypt top of Group E. A shock defeat to Uganda, however, brought the players back down to earth.

'There are no easy games,' Cúper reminded them angrily. 'We're not on our way to the World Cup yet, so FOCUS!'

A week later, Egypt faced Uganda again. Mohamed was ready to make things right. As his teammates moved the ball up the left wing, he looked for gaps in the Uganda defence. As soon as he spotted one, he burst forward, pointing for the pass.

'Now!'

When the pass arrived, Mohamed struck it first time on the volley. The keeper made a good save, but Mohamed scrambled the rebound over the goal-line.

Goooooooooooooooooooaaaaaaaaaaaaaaaaaallllllllllll llllllllllllllll!!!!!!!!!!!!!!!!!!!!

It certainly wasn't Mohamed's prettiest strike, but he didn't care about that. Not one bit! A goal was a goal, and this goal happened to be very, very important. One more win against Congo would be enough to take Egypt to the tournament in Russia. The players were so close to achieving their World Cup dream, so close...

'Stay focused out there,' Cúper warned them. 'It's not over until it's over!'

When Mohamed ran through and chipped the ball over the keeper, however, the people of Egypt went wild. They just couldn't help it.

Mohamed jumped over the advertising boards to celebrate with the fans behind the goal. Everyone wanted to hug and thank their national hero. Even the substitutes sprinted across the pitch to join the party.

'Come on, there's still thirty minutes to go!' Cúper shouted. 'FOCUS!'

Unfortunately, his players didn't listen. With five minutes to go, Arnold Bouka Moutou crept in at the back-post and equalised for Congo. 1–1!

The Borg El Arab Stadium fell silent. The Egypt
supporters sat with their heads in their hands.
Mohamed fell to the floor in despair. Had their
World Cup hopes just disappeared before their eyes?
No, he picked himself up and kept believing.

'Come on!' Mohamed shouted, signalling for the
fans to make more noise.

With him on the pitch, there was always hope.
In the ninety-fourth minute, Mahmoud Hassan was
brought down in the Congo box. *Penalty!*

Mohamed had been preparing for this moment
all his life. As he waited for the referee's whistle, he
looked down at the ball and then up at the target.
Just one kick – it was that simple.

Mohamed ran up and… sent the keeper the
wrong way again!

*Goooooooooooooooooooooaaaaaaaaaaaaaaaallllllllllll
llllllllllllll!!!!!!!!!!!!!!!!!!!!!*

He had done it, Egypt had done it – they were off
to the 2018 World Cup! The party started right there
in the stadium and carried on for days all over the
country.

With five goals and two assists, Mohamed was now an international superstar. He was too proud for words. Instead, he jogged around the field with his arms out wide like an aeroplane. It was like he was eight years old again, celebrating a Totti wondergoal on the pitch in Nagrig.

Even during the most amazing moments of his life, Mohamed always remembered how lucky he was. When he got the chance, he knelt down and kissed the ground below his feet. And when an Egyptian businessman offered him a luxury villa, Mohamed asked for the money to be donated to charity instead.

'Please give it to the people of Nagrig,' he said. 'They're the ones who need it most.'

That only made Egypt love him even more. In the elections for the nation's next president, over a million people added Mohamed's name and ticked the box. They were so proud of their humble hero, especially when he was named the 2017 African Footballer of the Year. He was the first Egyptian to win the award since Mahmoud El Khatib in 1983.

'I want to be the best player in the history of

Egyptian football,' Mohamed said in his acceptance speech, but he was just being modest. That title was already his, and he was still only twenty-five.

It was an unforgettable night for Mohamed. Not only did he win Player of the Year, but The Pharaohs won Team of the Year. That meant more to him than the individual award.

'Now, we just need to win the World Cup!' Mohamed told Elneny. Mohamed was smiling but he wasn't joking.

CHAPTER 22

LIVERPOOL

When Mohamed signed for Chelsea back in 2014, it was a bitter disappointment for Barry Hunter, Dave Fallows and Michael Edwards. Liverpool's top scouts had worked really hard to try and bring him to the club.

However, they didn't just give up and move on to another young talent. Instead, they watched and waited as Mohamed went off to Italy and became a star at Fiorentina and Roma. Unlike Chelsea, Liverpool weren't surprised at all.

'See, we were right about him!' the scouts told anyone who would listen. Among those who did listen was the new Liverpool manager, Jürgen Klopp.

Klopp already knew all about Mohamed's talent. He had first seen him play in a friendly between Basel and his previous club, Borussia Dortmund. It was a match that he would never forget.

'Wow, that guy is phenomenal!' Klopp thought to himself. His speed would suit Dortmund's style perfectly. But by the time he tried to buy him, Mohamed had already signed for Chelsea.

Everywhere Klopp went, the name 'Mohamed Salah' kept popping up. And it wasn't just Hunter, Fallows and Edwards who were talking about Mohamed; it was also the club's Italian scout, Paul Goldrick.

'Trust us, this guy will score goals!' he said with total confidence.

Klopp didn't need persuading. Liverpool were one top attacker away from a world-class frontline. He was sure that Mohamed would fit in brilliantly alongside Sadio Mané, Roberto Firmino and Philippe Coutinho.

'But would Roma sell him?' Klopp wondered. 'And would he want to join Liverpool?'

The answer to both questions was 'yes'. The Roma President James Pallotta wanted to keep Mohamed, but he couldn't say no to Liverpool's big-money offer: £37 million for a player who had cost Roma £13 million? That was a profit of £24 million!

'If Salah wants to leave, we won't stand in his way,' the club president announced.

Mohamed loved Roma – the city, the fans, the manager, his teammates. He was so thankful for all the love and support. Serie A would always have a special place in his heart. He didn't want to leave but, at the same time, this was a top Premier League club calling.

'I'm sorry but I can't say no to that,' he explained to Pallotta.

When he left Chelsea and moved to Italy, Mohamed always hoped that one day he would get a second chance in England. He had unfinished business. To most football fans there, he was just one of a long list of foreign failures who couldn't handle the pace and power of the Premier League. That wasn't true, though. Mohamed was determined to prove himself, and prove those other people wrong.

At Liverpool, he would have the chance to do just that. It was an amazing club, with an amazing history. As a teenager at El Mokawloon, Liverpool was his favourite team to play with on FIFA. Mohamed knew all the names – Steven Gerrard, Jamie Carragher, Xabi Alonso, Sami Hyypiä. Those heroes had won the Champions League in 2005.

'Hopefully, I can become an Anfield legend too!' he told Elneny excitedly.

Mohamed had played at Anfield only once before, for Chelsea, but he still remembered the incredible atmosphere in the stadium, and the famous 'This is Anfield' sign that all the Liverpool players touched. Their fans sang with so much passion, from the first minute to the last. 'You'll Never Walk Alone' gave him goosebumps every time. He couldn't wait to hear 'The Kop' chanting his name when he scored. It would be yet another dream come true.

'Welcome to Liverpool,' Klopp said with a big, warm smile on his face. 'At last, we get to work together!'

Mohamed got on well with his new boss straight away. Klopp, like Spalletti at Roma, was Mohamed's favourite kind of coach – a great man-manager who was eager to help him reach the next level.

'I want you to play higher up the pitch as a proper forward,' he told Mohamed. 'I know you scored a lot of goals at Roma, but we think you can score even more at Liverpool. We're going to turn you into a superstar!'

Mohamed loved the sound of that. He couldn't wait to get started. At his first training session at Melwood, he set out to impress his new teammates.

'I'm no Premier League flop!' Mohamed wanted to yell from the rooftops. But instead, he let his lethal left foot do the talking.

The Liverpool captain Jordan Henderson could remember watching Mohamed play for Chelsea. In his head, he pictured a small, skinny, skilful kid who looked a little lost in the limelight.

'I hope he's improved since then,' Jordan thought to himself.

This new teammate, however, seemed like a

totally different footballer. Mohamed looked strong and confident as he strolled out onto the Liverpool training pitch. His smile was gentle but if you looked a little closer, there was a fire burning in his eyes.

Once the training session started, Mohamed burst into action, running rings around the defenders. Dejan Lovren and Alberto Moreno were looking for a nice easy return after the summer break but they were in for a big shock. By the end of training, they needed another holiday to recover from Mohamed's masterclass.

Jordan turned to Adam Lallana and smiled. 'Wow, he's a top, top player!'

Mohamed scored on his Liverpool debut in a preseason friendly against Wigan Athletic. Roberto spotted Mohamed in space on the right. The pass was simple and so was Mohamed's finish.

Goooooooooooooooooooooaaaaaaaaaaaaaaaalllllllllllll lllllllllllllll!!!!!!!!!!!!!!!!!!!!

Wigan's DW Stadium was half-empty but the Liverpool fans still made plenty of noise for their new signing. Mohamed ran over to high-five Roberto.

'Welcome to the team!' Roberto cheered happily.

'Thanks, mate!' Mohamed cheered back.

Mohamed scored on his Premier League debut for Liverpool too. Their new-look attack clicked straight away. Together, they offered such a dangerous mix of speed and skill. Sadio scored the first goal and Roberto scored the second from the penalty spot after a foul on Mohamed.

'Mo, it's your turn to score now!' Sadio joked.

Two minutes later, Roberto chipped the ball over the goalkeeper's head. Was it going in? No, but Mohamed sprinted into the six-yard box and tapped it home.

Goooooooooooooooooooaaaaaaaaaaaaaaaaalllllllllllll llllllllllll!!!!!!!!!!!!!!!!!!

This time, Watford's Vicarage Road Stadium was full and the Liverpool fans went wild. Roberto lifted Mohamed into the air.

'You're really part of the team now!' he cheered happily.

Mohamed was delighted. Thanks to his awesome new teammates, he was settling in really quickly at

Liverpool. And things were about to get even better when Arsenal came to Anfield.

Joe Gomez crossed from the right and Roberto headed it in. *1–0!*

Sadio cut in from the left and curled a shot into the bottom corner. *2–0!*

'Mo, it's your turn to score now!' he joked.

Mohamed was desperate to add his name to the scoresheet. It would be his first goal at Anfield, the moment that every new Liverpool player looked forward to.

In the second half, all the Arsenal defenders went up for a corner, except Héctor Bellerín. As the clearance came out to him, Bellerín's first touch was heavy, way too heavy when Mohamed was around. He headed the ball past Bellerín and chased after it.

Go on, Salah! Come on!

With the Liverpool fans urging him on, Mohamed sprinted all the way from his own half into the Arsenal penalty area in seven seconds. When he got there, he slowed down for the one-on-one. He couldn't waste another glorious chance; he should already have scored a hat-trick.

'Superstars almost always make the right decision'
– that's what Spalletti had told him.

Go on, Salah! Come on!

It was time for Mohamed to show the composure
he'd worked on since his days at Chelsea. He needed
to stay calm and score. Klopp believed in him and
so did everyone else at Liverpool. Mohamed guided
the ball around the goalkeeper and into the bottom
corner.

*Goooooooooooooooooooooaaaaaaaaaaaaaaaalllllllllllll
lllllllllllllll!!!!!!!!!!!!!!!!!!!!*

Anfield had a new hero.

CHAPTER 23

PREMIER LEAGUE PLAYER OF THE YEAR

We've got Salah, do do do do do do!
Mané Mané, do do do do do,
And Bobby Firmino,
And we sold Coutinho!

In January 2018, Liverpool's fab four became 'The Big Three' instead. Everyone was sad to see Philippe go to Barcelona but there was still plenty of attacking talent in the team. Sadio had five Premier League goals, Roberto had nine, and Mohamed had seventeen! Liverpool already had a new superstar to replace Philippe.

Mo Salah, Mo Salah
Running down the wing,

Salah la la la la la la
Egyptian King!

Once Mohamed started scoring, he couldn't stop! He was only one goal behind Tottenham's sharpshooter Harry Kane.

'If you carry on like this, you could break the Premier League record!' Jordan told him.

And Mohamed should have scored even more. He still had nightmares about the missed chances against the Manchester clubs. Why hadn't he been more clinical in the crucial moments? That was what being a superstar was all about. Mohamed could have won those big games for Liverpool but instead, City thrashed them 5–0 and United left Anfield with a draw.

'Don't worry, you're still learning,' Klopp had reassured him. 'Just keep doing what you're doing!'

Mohamed had bounced back in style, scoring two against West Ham, two against Southampton, two against Stoke City, and one against his old club, Chelsea. He had also won the Premier League Player of the Month awards for November *and* December.

Mohamed had been looking forward to the rematch with Manchester City for months. Pep Guardiola's team were fifteen points clear at the top of the table and they hadn't lost a Premier League match all season. It was the perfect opportunity for Mohamed to prove that he *was* a big game player. His club was counting on him and this time, he wouldn't let the fans down.

At half-time, it was 1–1 but in the second half, 'The Big Three' took over.

Roberto lobbed the keeper. *2–1!*

Mohamed stole the ball off Nicolás Otamendi and passed to Sadio on the edge of the box. *Bang – 3–1!*

'Thanks!' Sadio cheered, giving his friend a high-five. 'Mo, it's your turn to score now!'

A few minutes later, Ederson, the Manchester City goalkeeper, cleared the ball straight to Mohamed. Was this his big chance? He was a long way from goal but it was worth a try. He was full of confidence and the Liverpool fans were urging him on.

Shoot! Shoot! Shoot!

Why not? Mohamed curled the ball over

Ederson's head and it bounced down into the back of the net. *4–1!*

Goooooooooooooooooooaaaaaaaaaaaaaaaalllllllllllll llllllllllllll!!!!!!!!!!!!!!!!!!!!

The party started early at Anfield. Klopp ran up and down the touchline, punching the air. What a performance from his strikeforce!

Out on the pitch, Mohamed punched the air too. Usually, he celebrated calmly but he was really fired up for the big game. Finally, he had his revenge.

'That's more like it!' Mohamed snarled. For once, he wasn't smiling at all.

Forget Barcelona's 'MSN' or Real Madrid's 'BBC' – Liverpool's 'Big Three' were the new hottest strikeforce in the world.

'We're like Brazil's 3 Rs,' Mohamed laughed, thinking back to his childhood heroes. 'I'm Ronaldo!'

They weren't just scoring goals in the Premier League; they were scoring goals in the Champions League too.

In the group stage, they had hit seven past Maribor and another seven past Spartak Moscow. But would the goals dry up now that Philippe was gone?

No way! In the Round of 16 match away at Porto, 'The Big Three' took over again.

Sadio's shot squirmed through the keeper's hands. *1–0!*

James Milner's strike hit the post and bounced back to Mohamed. He flicked the ball over the diving goalkeeper, juggled it on his head and then steered it past the diving defender. *2–0!*

This time, Mohamed celebrated with a huge grin on his face. It was his thirtieth goal of the season, and there were still two whole months to go!

. In the second half, Roberto's shot was saved but the rebound fell to Sadio. *3–0!*

James crossed to Roberto. *4–0!*

It was game over but Liverpool still weren't finished. They were hungry for more. Sadio completed his hat-trick with a long-range rocket. *5–0!*

Liverpool cruised into the Champions League quarter-finals, where they would face... Manchester City again! The pressure was on but Mohamed was feeling really positive.

'If we play like we did against Porto, we can beat anyone!' he cheered.

The atmosphere at Anfield was absolutely electric. On big European nights like this, players could become legends with one kick of the ball. Who would Liverpool's hero be?

Mohamed dribbled into the City half and slipped a lovely pass into Roberto's path. Ederson saved his shot but Roberto managed to poke the rebound across to Mohamed. Six yards out and on his lethal left foot; there was no way he was going to miss.

Gooooooooooooooooooooaaaaaaaaaaaaaaaallllllllllll llllllllllllll!!!!!!!!!!!!!!!!!!

As Mohamed slid across the Anfield grass, the Liverpool fans bounced up and down in the stands. Oh, how they loved their Egyptian King!

Alex Oxlade-Chamberlain got the second goal, and Sadio got the third from Mohamed's teasing cross. 'The Big Three' were simply unstoppable.

'Great work, guys!' Roberto cried out as they shared a group hug.

They still had a long way to go, however. In the

second leg in Manchester, City took the lead in the second minute. Suddenly, the Liverpool players and fans looked anxious. What they needed was a cool head to save the day...

Mohamed passed to Sadio, who dribbled into the City penalty area. Ederson came out to stop him but he couldn't hold it. Mohamed was on to the loose ball in a flash. He poked it away from the goalkeeper and then dinked it over the defender's head.

Gooooooooooooooooooooaaaaaaaaaaaaaaaallllllllllllll lllllllllllllll!!!!!!!!!!!!!!!!!!!

So calm and so classy! Mohamed ran over to the ecstatic Liverpool fans and stood in front of them with his arms out wide, enjoying his superstar moment. He hoped that the people of Nagrig were enjoying it too, on the TV screen at the local café.

Mo Salah, Mo Salah
Running down the wing,
Salah la la la la la la
Egyptian King!

'Surely, life doesn't get any better than this!' he thought to himself.

But amazingly, it did. After beating Manchester
City, Liverpool then beat Mohamed's old club, Roma.
They were through to the Champions League final!

'You legend!' Jordan shouted, lifting Mohamed
high into the air. Mohamed was now up to forty-
three goals in all competitions.

The last team standing in Liverpool's way were
the thirteen-time European Champions, Real Madrid.
The newspapers were calling it the 'Battle of the
Superstars', Mohamed vs Ronaldo, but Mohamed
was a humble hero.

'It's all about the team,' he kept saying in every
interview, even when he won the PFA Premier
League Player of the Year award.

'I always think about the team, not about myself,'
Mohamed said in his acceptance speech. 'So, the
most important thing for me is to win something
with the team.'

Lifting the Champions League trophy would be
a fairy-tale ending to Mohamed's fairy-tale season.
Would he freeze on the big stage in Kyiv, or would
he lead Liverpool to victory yet again?

For the first twenty-seven minutes, the match was tense and end-to-end. Liverpool's 'Big Three' looked as dangerous as ever but that was all about to change.

Sergio Ramos marked Mohamed tightly, following him all over the pitch. He was a tough defender to shake off but Mohamed tried his hardest. As they battled for the ball, Ramos dragged him to the ground.

'Argghhhhh!' Mohamed screamed in agony, clutching his shoulder.

The match carried on, but he stayed down. Was Mohamed's Champions League final over already? No, he couldn't give up yet. The physio helped him up and he jogged back on to the pitch, but the pain was too much. A minute later, Mohamed fell to the ground again and this time, the tears streamed down his cheeks.

'I'm sorry, mate,' Sadio said, putting an arm around his shoulder. 'We'll do our best to win it without you!'

Sadly, Real Madrid were just too strong for them.

It was a heartbreaking way for Mohamed's season to end, but he had so much to feel proud of.

No, he hadn't yet won any of Europe's top team trophies but there would be plenty of time for that. In the meantime, Mohamed was the African Footballer of the Year, the PFA Premier League Player of the Year and the Premier League Golden Boot winner, with a record thirty-two goals.

Not bad for a 'Premier League flop'. Four years after his Chelsea disappointment, Mohamed had returned to England as a completely different footballer at Liverpool – older, wiser and a whole lot better. It had taken a lot of hard work and team work, but Mohamed was now a world-class superstar, hot on the heels of Ronaldo and Messi.

And as Mohamed's old El Mokawloon coach Hamdi Nooh liked to say, 'Superstars never stop improving.' Defences of the world – be warned!

Turn the page for a sneak preview of
another brilliant football story by
Matt and Tom Oldfield. . .

DE BRUYNE

CHAPTER 1

MANCHESTER CITY'S MAIN MAN

Stamford Bridge, 30 September 2017

There was great excitement all across the footballing world, but especially around the Stamford Bridge stadium in West London. It was a sell-out for the biggest game of the Premier League season so far – the champions, Chelsea, versus the most entertaining team in England, Manchester City.

So, who would win the battle of the best? Which manager would come out on top: Chelsea's Antonio Conte or City's Pep Guardiola? And which brilliant Belgian would shine the brightest: Chelsea's Eden Hazard or City's midfield maestro, Kevin De Bruyne?

For Kevin, the match meant more than just another three points for his team. Back in 2012, at the age of twenty, he had made the bold move from his Belgian club Genk to Chelsea, with high hopes of becoming 'the next Frank Lampard', or even 'the new Zinedine Zidane'.

Kevin's manager at Chelsea José Mourinho had promised him game-time but, instead, he spent two seasons either out on loan, or sat on the bench. Kevin had always been a stubborn star. He was impatient and strong-willed too. When he saw that he had no chance at Chelsea, he decided to make a name for himself somewhere else. He went to Germany and quickly became 'The King of the Assists' at VfL Wolfsburg.

Now, Kevin was back in England, starring for a new club. He was the best player in the Premier League and Manchester City were the best team too. Kevin had no hard feelings towards his old club but nevertheless, he had a point to prove to some people. It was time to show, once and for all, that he wasn't a 'Chelsea flop'. Five years on, Kevin was a completely different playmaker – older, wiser, and a whole lot better.

'Let's win this, lads!' his captain David Silva clapped and cheered before kick-off.

That wouldn't be easy away at Stamford Bridge, but City were top of the table and playing with so much style and confidence. With Kevin starting every attack in central midfield, Pep's grand plan was working brilliantly. City had thrashed Liverpool 5–0, then Watford 6–0, then Crystal Palace 5–0. Could they thrash Chelsea too?

Kevin dropped deep to get the ball as often as possible. He had two fantastic feet, capable of creating magic. Sometimes, he curled beautiful long passes over the top for City's speedy winger Raheem Sterling to chase. Sometimes, he played clever one-twos with Raheem, David and right-back Kyle Walker. Sometimes he was on the right, sometimes he was on the left, and sometimes he was in the middle. Kevin was everywhere, doing everything to help his team to win.

His first chance to score came from a free kick.

He had scored plenty in his career, even one against Barcelona in the Champions League. This time, however, his Belgian international teammate Thibaut Courtois made a comfortable save.

'Aaaaaaaaaahhhhhhhhh,' the City fans let out a groan of disappointment, like the air escaping from a balloon. Kevin was so talented that they expected him to get it right every time.

'Next time,' he thought to himself as he ran back into position. As the game went on, Kevin, and City, got better and better.

CHANCE! Kevin crossed to Gabriel Jesus but it was intercepted by a Chelsea defender.

CHANCE! Kevin delivered a dangerous corner kick but Gabriel headed wide.

CHANCE! Kevin chipped the ball towards Gabriel but he headed wide again.

The City fans were growing restless in their seats. Their team was creating lots and lots of chances – but without their star striker, Sergio Agüero, who was going to step up and score the winning goal?

Playing in his new deeper midfield role, Kevin

hadn't scored yet that season. Pep wanted him to be the team's pass-master, using his amazing X-ray vision to set up goals for other players. But what if they couldn't score?

Kevin could strike a brilliant shot, full of power and swerve. Like his hero Zidane, he was the complete midfielder, and he was determined to prove himself as a big game player. A win against Chelsea would keep City top of the Premier League, above their local rivals, Manchester United. His team needed him more than ever...

'Attack!' Pep shouted from the sidelines. 'Attack!'

So, the next time that Kevin played a quick pass to Gabriel, he kept running forward for the one-two. Kevin got the ball back and burst through the Chelsea midfield. He was just outside the penalty area now, with plenty of space to...

'Shoot!' the City fans urged. 'Shoot!'

It was on his left foot but Kevin didn't really have a weaker foot, just two magic wands. He steadied himself, pulled his leg back and struck the ball sweetly. Abracadabra! It flew through the air and over Courtois' outstretched arms.

Goooooooooooooooooooaaaaaaaaaaaaaaaalllllllllllll lllllllllllll!!!!!!!!!!!!!!!!!!!!

'DE BRUYNE!!' the TV commentator cried out. 'Oh, that's special!'

What an important goal! As the ball hit the back of the net, the City supporters went wild. Kevin ran towards them, shaking his finger and roaring like a lion. He was so pumped up with pride and joy. He wanted to win the Premier League title so much.

On the touchline, Pep punched the air with delight. Their Brazilian substitute Danilo couldn't contain his excitement. He ran straight onto the pitch to bump chests with their hero. Soon, Kevin was at the centre of a big team hug.

'Come on!' he called out to the supporters and, in reply, they sang their favourite song:

Ohhhhhhhh! Kevin De Bruyne!
Ohhhhhhhh! Kevin De Bruyne!

It was an amazing moment for Manchester City's main man, one that he would never forget. Kevin had scored his team's winning goal, and against

Chelsea! It didn't get any better than that. Back at Stamford Bridge, the Belgian had showed the world that he was now a superstar.

'Kev, you're the best!' his manager Pep Guardiola said with a huge smile on his face.

Mourinho might not have believed in him at Chelsea, but Guardiola certainly did at Manchester City. And most importantly, Kevin believed in himself. He had always known that he had the talent, the drive and the resilience to reach the very top, even during his early days in Drongen.

Basel
🏆 Swiss Super League: 2012–13

Liverpool
🏆 UEFA Champions League runner-up: 2017–18

Egypt
🏆 Africa Cup of Nations runner-up: 2017

Egypt
🏆 CAF Most Promising Talent of the Year: 2012
🏆 A.S. Roma Player of the Season: 2015–16
🏆 CAF Team of the Year: 2016, 2017

- 🏆 CAF Africa Cup of Nations Team of the Tournament: 2017
- 🏆 PFA Player of the Month: November 2017, December 2017, February 2018, March 2018
- 🏆 African Footballer of the Year: 2017
- 🏆 BBC African Footballer of the Year: 2017
- 🏆 PFA Players' Player of the Year: 2017–18
- 🏆 FWA Footballer of the Year: 2017–18
- 🏆 Premier League Golden Boot: 2017–18
- 🏆 Premier League Player of the Season: 2017–18
- 🏆 PFA Team of the Year: 2017–18 Premier League

SALAH

(11) THE FACTS

NAME: MOHAMED SALAH GHALY

DATE OF BIRTH: 15 June 1992

AGE: 26

PLACE OF BIRTH: Nagrig

NATIONALITY: Egypt

BEST FRIEND: Mohamed Elneny

CURRENT CLUB: Liverpool

POSITION: RW

THE STATS

Height (cm):	175
Club appearances:	303
Club goals:	121
Club trophies:	1
International appearances:	57
International goals:	33
International trophies:	0
Ballon d'Ors:	0

★ ★ ★ **HERO RATING: 90** ★ ★ ★

GREATEST MOMENTS

Type and search the web links to see the magic for yourself!

1 25 DECEMBER 2010, AL AHLY 5–1 EL MOKAWLOON

https://www.youtube.com/watch?v=f–labUbSHNQ
Mohamed's first senior goal for El Mokawloon came against the Egyptian Champions, Al Ahly. It had all the features of a classic Salah strike. Mohamed used his amazing sprint speed to race past the defence and his composure to find the net. Yes, maybe the goalkeeper should have done better, but Mohamed wasn't yet the sharpshooter he is now!

26 JULY 2012,
BRAZIL 3–2 EGYPT

https://www.youtube.com/watch?v=SqUmUBBR5kI
The London Olympics in 2012 was a special tournament
for Mohamed. He scored three goals in Egypt's first
three games, including this one against Brazil. He was
surrounded by three defenders but with two magical
touches, he created enough space to score. That goal
proved that Mohamed belonged at the top level.

26 NOVEMBER 2013,
BASEL 1–0 CHELSEA

https://www.youtube.com/watch?v=oAbVLWsEUrY&t=1s
Mohamed scored three goals in four European games for
Basel against Chelsea, but this was the pick of the bunch.
With five minutes to go, the score was still 0–0. Step
forward Mohamed, a new European star. He controlled
a long ball beautifully, dribbled into the penalty area, and
lifted his shot over the goalkeeper. Two months later,
Mohamed was a Chelsea player.

4   8 OCTOBER 2013, EGYPT 2–1 CONGO

https://www.youtube.com/watch?v=UEs7EMWAOLg

This was the day Mohamed confirmed his place as Egypt's national hero by leading them to the 2018 World Cup. He scored both of his team's goals but the second is the one everyone will remember. In the ninety-fourth minute, Egypt won a penalty and Mohamed stepped up and scored the winner.

5   24 APRIL 2018, LIVERPOOL 5–2 ROMA

https://www.youtube.com/watch?v=ltd5JqbVaVw

This was an emotional night for Mohamed, playing against his old club in the Champions League semi-final. However, he kept a cool head as always. His first goal was a curling strike from the edge of the area, and his second was a delicate dink over the goalkeeper. He rounded off a world-class performance by setting up his 'Big Three' partners, Sadio Mané and Roberto Firmino.

PLAY LIKE YOUR HEROES

MOHAMED SALAH'S DELICATE DINK

SEE IT HERE You Tube

https://www.youtube.com/watch?v=4pgFE8PBEyk

STEP 1: Get some good teammates! They don't have to be as talented as Mané and Firmino, but you're going to need some help here.

STEP 2: Wait until your teammate gets the ball and then burst forward as fast as you can. Remember to time your run and stay onside.

STEP 3: If you've got amazing sprint speed like Mohamed, no-one is going to catch you. But if not, use your skill to dance past any last defenders.

STEP 4: Dribble forward into the penalty area. The closer you are to goal, the more likely you are to score. No heavy touches, though!

STEP 5: Keep your cool! You're one-on-one with the goalkeeper now, and it's all about composure.

TEST YOUR KNOWLEDGE

QUESTIONS

1. Name three of Mohamed's childhood football heroes.

2. What was the name of the boy who Reda El-Mallah was supposed to be scouting in Nagrig?

3. What position did Mohamed first play in the El Mokawloon youth team?

4. Which team did Mohamed like to play with on FIFA as a teenager?

5. How old was Mohamed when he made his first-team debut for El Mokawloon?

6. How old was Mohamed when he made his senior debut for Egypt?

7. What was the reason for Mohamed's first trip to London?

8. How many goals did Mohamed score for Basel in his four games against Chelsea?

9. Who was the Chelsea manager who brought Mohamed to Stamford Bridge?

10. Who are the other two members of Liverpool's 'Big Three'?

11. How many Premier League goals did Mohamed score in the 2017–18 season?

Answers below. . . No cheating!

1. *Any of Zinedine Zidane, Ryan Giggs, Francesco Totti, Ronaldo, Rivaldo and Ronaldinho.* 2. *Sherif* 3. *Left-back* 4. *Liverpool* 5. *Sixteen* 6. *Nineteen* 7. *He played for Egypt at the 2012 Olympics.* 8. *Three* 9. *José Mourinho* 10. *Sadio Mané and Roberto Firmino* 11. *Thirty-two*

HAVE YOU GOT THEM ALL?

FOOTBALL HEROES